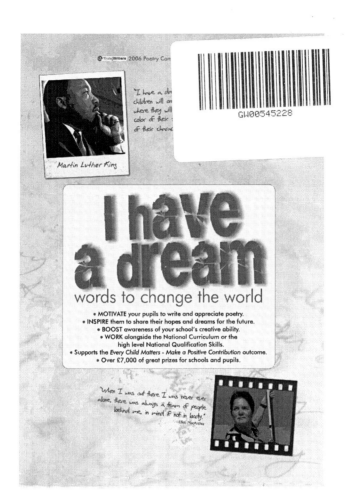

Young Writers 2006 Poetry Competition

"I have a dr
children will on
where they will
color of their
of their charac

Martin Luther King

I have a dream

words to change the world

- MOTIVATE your pupils to write and appreciate poetry.
- INSPIRE them to share their hopes and dreams for the future.
- BOOST awareness of your school's creative ability.
- WORK alongside the National Curriculum or the
  high level National Qualification Skills.
- Supports the *Every Child Matters - Make a Positive Contribution* outcome.
- Over £7,000 of great prizes for schools and pupils.

"When I was out there I was never ever
alone, there was always a team of people
behind me, in mind if not in body."
— Ellen MacArthur

Central Southern England
Edited by Mark Richardson

 Young**Writers**

First published in Great Britain in 2006 by:
Young Writers
Remus House
Coltsfoot Drive
Peterborough
PE2 9JX
Telephone: 01733 890066
Website: www.youngwriters.co.uk

SB ISBN 1 84602 501 X

Foreword

Imagine a teenager's brain; a fertile yet fragile expanse teeming with ideas, aspirations, questions and emotions. Imagine a classroom full of racing minds, scratching pens writing an endless stream of ideas and thoughts . . .

. . . Imagine your words in print reaching a wider audience. Imagine that maybe, just maybe, your words can make a difference. Strike a chord. Touch a life. Change the world. Imagine no more . . .

'I Have a Dream' is a series of poetry collections written by 11 to 18-year-olds from schools and colleges across the UK and overseas. Pupils were invited to send us their poems using the theme 'I I lave a Dream'. Selected entries range from dreams they've experienced to childhood fantasies of stardom and wealth, through inspirational poems of their dreams for a better future and of people who have influenced and inspired their lives.

The series is a snapshot of who and what inspires, influences and enthuses young adults of today. It shows an insight into their hopes, dreams and aspirations of the future and displays how their dreams are an escape from the pressures of today's modern life. Young Writers are proud to present this anthology, which is truly inspired and sure to be an inspiration to all who read it.

Contents

Raffaella Parente (13)	56
Laura Turnbull (12)	57
Carol Leonard (12)	57
Amanda Leslie (13)	58
Louisa Clark (12)	59
Alysha Elkins-Green (13)	59
Kirsty Towes (14)	60
Natalie Burgess (12)	61
Kelly Lord (12)	61
Julia Tansley (11)	62
Abigail Pollard (11)	63
Jessica Chapman (12)	64
Nicola Kennedy (12)	65
Lucy Croker (11)	66
Emma Nias (12)	66
Aimee Azhar (11)	67
Rebecca Williams (14)	67
Emma Gray (12)	68
Karly Masters (11)	68
Sarah Meeking (12)	69
Beth MacDonald (12)	69
Demi Mantell (13)	70
Amy Zimmermann (11)	71
Heather Dolan (12)	72
Charlotte Inge (12)	73
Amy O'Connor (12)	74
Annie Nye (12)	74
Clare Hurst (12)	75
Daisy Keeling (11)	75
Victoria Sillett (12)	76
Safiyah Dinaully (11)	77
Jade Wilkinson (12)	77
Lucy Bushell (12)	78
Hannah Wheatley (11)	78
Alexandra Bohan (13)	79
Tessa Smith (13)	79
Elizabeth Hillman (11)	80
Abbie Jenkins (13)	80
Nicola Dyer (12)	81
Katy Rode (13)	81
Emma Redgrove (13)	82
Catherine Pickett 13)	83

Imogen Hay (13)	83
Stephanie Moir (12)	84
Miriam Playfoot (12)	84
Jasmine Hutchings (13)	85
Flisa Lawrance (12)	85
Kayleigh Fuller (13)	86
Harriet Lloyd (13)	87
Gail Betts (12)	88
Daniela Defeo (13)	89
Harriette Wysocki (13)	90
Zoe Turner (13)	91

Newlands School, Seaford

Tom Pearce (13)	91
Anna Giles (14)	92
James O'Donnell (12)	93
Timothy Waters (13)	94
Saskia Gunson (14)	94
Francesca Forde (13)	95
Philip Hersee (13)	95
Katy Feek (14)	96
Nalissa Petfield (12)	97
Nina Wiehrich (13)	97
Vicky Cowlett (12)	98
Georgia Hunt (12)	98
Rachel Bonnici (12)	99
Chloë Sanders (12)	99
Jasmine Munns (12)	100

Owlswick School, Lewes

Billy George (13)	100
Matthew Kemp (14)	101

Park College, Eastbourne

Rebecca Santos (18)	102

Patcham House Special School, Brighton

Rosemary Whitney (16)	103

St Leonard's Mayfield School, Mayfield

Alice Phillips (14)	104
Liza Baucher (14)	105
Sophie Bowe (13)	106
Charlotte Hutchinson (14)	107
Alice Voke (13)	108
Eleanor McLaren (13)	109
Sefi Bagshawe (14)	110
Lucy Melia (12)	111
Alice Holden (13)	112
Amber Gill (13)	113
Helen Bowen Wright (13)	113
Katie Grainger (11)	114
Isobel Bushell (13)	115
Alice Saldanha (11)	116
Rosie Gaston (11)	117
Emma Graham (13)	118
Lily Cottle (11)	119

Sandford Middle School, Wareham

Emily Wright (13)	120
Jake Muscato (11)	120
Courtney Best (12)	121
Mike Rice (12)	121
Henry Watkins (12)	122
Monica Bollani (13)	123
Tom Rolls (12)	124
Lauren Adams (13)	125
Ryan King (12)	125
Stephen Pope (12)	126
William Foster (12)	126
Ben Honeywill (12)	127
Oliver Walters (12)	127
Layla Norris (13)	128
Becky Maidment (13)	129
Jack Harcourt (11)	130
Anton Appleton (12)	131
Thomas Houlding (12)	132
Melanie Welsh (12)	132
Rosie Coombs (12)	133
Jack Cullimore (12)	133

Danielle Hewitt (12)	134
Nicola Parry (11)	134
Kerry Jarvis (12)	135
Carly-Jade Mason (11)	135
Anna Rowe (12)	136
Lauren Holder (13)	137
Rebecca Howman (13)	138
Elisha Tagart (13)	139
Matt Sadler (12)	139
Ben Davies (12)	140
Katie England (12)	141
Amelia Elms (12)	142
Chloe Spore (12)	143
Lucy Barfoot (11)	144
Alex Boyd (12)	145
Emily Witham (11)	146
Steven Churchill (12)	147
Michael Goff (11)	148
Kayleigh Noyce (13)	148
Robert Spivey (11)	149
Esmé Phillips (12)	149
Ben Newton (13)	150
Jenna Dick (12)	151
Nat Scott (13)	151
Ryan Pannell (12)	152
Sophie Terrell (13)	153
Catherine Atwell (12)	154
Stacey Watkins (12)	155
Liam Sykes (13)	155
Bethany Willmot (13)	156
Daisy Brock (13)	157
Lauren Peters (12)	158
Emily Gale (12)	159
Gareth Eyles (12)	160
Emma Vinson (13)	161
Tanya Watkins (13)	162
Courtney Critchell (12)	163
Emily Crocker (13)	164
Rebecca Burt (12)	165
Briony Wills (12)	166

The Cavendish School, Eastbourne

The Poems

Ali

He would float like a butterfly,
He would sting like a bee
He is my inspiration,
Muhammad Ali.

From the words of his mouth the most power came,
Not from the gloves he put on, again and again.
The speeches he made and the way he delivered,
He said what he felt and he never dithered.

Against the war in Nam, and he made it known,
And for this, great hatred he was shown.
But he always spoke out and was never one to mumble,
And for this I respect him more than for his 'Rumble In The Jungle'.

With an old zimmer frame he slowly makes his way,
Not with the speed of his former days.
His hands grip to the cold dull frame,
These hands are the same ones which brought so much fame.

But his eyes reveal the man inside,
The man who never tried to hide.
Hide away from the reality, the fire,
The fire inside which we've all come to admire.

The same fire that brought giants down to their knees,
Sonny Liston, George Foreman and the rest all agree,
He's an inspiration for you and for me,
This is the legend of Muhammad Ali.

He would float like a butterfly,
He would sting like a bee.
Ho is my inspiration,
Muhammad Ali.

Henry Davies (14)
Eastbourne College, Eastbourne

I Wish

I wish we could live in a world of peace
I wish that poverty and suffering will cease
I wish that there were no battles or wars
I wish that weaponry could be used for a better cause
I wish

I wish to get rid of all disease
I wish not to let people on the streets, freeze
I wish for no more drugs
I wish for no more thugs
I wish

I wish for no more robbery
I wish for no stealing of famous pottery
I wish for no more murders
I wish for no more burglars

I wish
I wish
I wish.

Will Francis (14)
Eastbourne College, Eastbourne

Artificial

To follow in your friends' conversation,
To be afraid to voice your own opinion,
To be stranded, alone in the corner,
Then to involve yourself in chatter,
Then to stand in a crowd and speak out,
Then to become accepted amongst one another

Was a feign outlook on life.

How many people spoke to her,
Presuming what she presumed
And carried out what she did!

Sophie Upfield (15)
Eastbourne College, Eastbourne

Things Around Us

Look down on the Earth and up at the sky,
Who made all this and why?

Look at the flowers, aren't they nice?
That's all someone needs and it will suffice.

Taste the fresh fruit, they are sweet,
It all comes with colours, how neat!

Hear the different sounds, provoke your senses
They can calm and excite any in presence.

Smell for your joy, but don't get hooked
There are many out there, don't overlook.

These beautiful things, do they come by chance?
Look around you, only a glance.

Turn from the darkness and look, taste and hear
Glory to Him who made it clear.

Roydon Tse (14)
Eastbourne College, Eastbourne

Every Door Is Open

When you are young, life could be the sun,
Shining so bright, so full of hopes, so full of dreams,
Every door is open, you have so many chances,
But it's not always as bright as it seems.

We grow old like the waves of the sea,
Washing in and out with the tides,
The years come and go just as easily,
So soon we find all our dreams have died.

When our life is over and our time is spent,
We only think of our dreams that have gone,
Instead we ought to look back on our life,
And feel good for the things we have done.

Charlotte Tickle (14)
Eastbourne College, Eastbourne

You

Look around you, what do you see?
Is this what you wanted, is this your dream?

See what you have created, is it really fair
To see so much pain, hurt and despair?

You are the owner and we are the keepers,
How could you do this? It's hard to decipher.

Does it pain you to see the damage, do you weep,
As you gaze down upon this wreckage that we have to keep?

Are you powerless to stop it, or do you have the power
As we remain waiting for our final hour?

As we wait for your answer, what shall we expect,
Will you give us another reason to regret?

My time has come and I have to go,
I waited for you but you were too slow.

I have long gone but still remember this,
You will be the one that I will not miss.

I left this place sad and with a dream . . .
But now it's washed up along with me.

Look around you, what do you see?
Is this still what you wanted; is this still your dream?

Yasaman Tehrani (14)
Eastbourne College, Eastbourne

If You Can . . .

If you can stand up for your own rights,
If you can speak out loud,
If you're not scared to put up a fight,
If you can stand out in a crowd.

If you know how it feels to be free,
If you can tell the truth in any case.
If you can break the chains that'll set you free,
If you can stand up and face.

If you can battle on through pain and love,
If you want a say; say it clear.
If you aim to achieve high and above,
If you say it for the whole world to hear.

If you can say you love your friends,
If you can learn to let people in,
If you can learn to make amends,
If you can cleanse away your sin.

If in yourself, you really believe,
If you set out to achieve,
If you don't judge people, then you would see,
That everyone in our world should be free.

Charlie Hugill (15)
Eastbourne College, Eastbourne

Fallout

And will we ever sing again?
Will grass be green
And animals lean?
I sigh for the people who ask this;
'Will we ever sing again?'

Men used to live here once
But now they live below
Below.

I watch from above
I am wind, rain, cold and heat
I see all,
Control all.

Rain is my tears
I weep
I weep
For the men and women
Whom I created.

They destroyed everything, pure and clean;
Woods, water, air
Animals die of poison
Worm to bear.

This war they call it
Makes me sad.
No one should live beneath the ground.

Charlie Harding (13)
Eastbourne College, Eastbourne

Democracy?

First they stole our fox-hunting
We did not notice
Because we live in a democracy.

Then they stole our right to a trial
We did not notice
Because we live in a democracy.

Then they stole our smoky pubs
We did not notice
Because we live in a democracy.

Then they stole our identity
We did not notice
Because we live in a democracy.

So when Big Brother arrived
We could not notice
As we had forgotten the meaning of democracy.

Edward Hickman Casey (14)
Eastbourne College, Eastbourne

Unseen

To hide away behind those you admire.
To take their footsteps, every step you walk.
To dream their dreams when that's not what you're wishing,
To love the ones they love, who love them, not you.

To do your hair the way other women do theirs.
To colour your eyes as black as thunder clouds,
To follow rules that others set out for you,
To be as quiet as the quietest little mouse.

To agree but now deep down, you disagree.
What will you do when they all up and leave?
You must stand up for all that you believe,
For to be alone but true, is greater than unseen.

Katy Dougal (15)
Eastbourne College, Eastbourne

Bullies

I wish they'd treat me equally, I wish they'd treat me equally
I wish they'd treat me fair
I wish they'd feel melancholy, when they forgot to care
When they forgot to care

They fought me and they beat me
Yet they will never understand
I'm not the bum, the freak, the idiot
Just because they so demand

They might have hurt me purposely
They might have pulled me down
I'll never lose my spirit though
I'll always stand my ground

Though they often disappointed me
And often made me scared
I'd be happy if they thought
And say sorry, if they dared.

Baika Altymuhammedov (15)
Eastbourne College, Eastbourne

World Poverty

People stop, stand and stare,
These are the people who despair.
Under the harsh and burning sun
There is no food, there is none.

Cracked dry ground beneath their toes,
In a field, blank, where nothing grows.
Life seems to fall down an increasing slope,
But them, they grasp onto hope.

But who can help, who can there be?
I'll tell you my friend, it is you and me!

Ed Coates (15)
Eastbourne College, Eastbourne

Inspirational Poem

They keep giving me drugs, tablets and pills,
Injections and blood tests, that's all I get.
Why can't they leave me, give me a break,
Please leave me alone, just for a while.
I need to have fun, like all my friends,
Be part of the group, fit in with the crowd.
Sometimes I'm high, sometimes I'm low,
But I know I'll make it, through thick and thin.

I've done it! I've made it! I'm out of this mess,
I'm clear at last, free to go.
I'll never go back, keep going forward,
Will never again take my life for granted.
Now I can go and hold my head high,
With relief in my heart and a spring in my step.
An experience that will be with me,
I'll never forget.

Hannah Wenham (14)
Eastbourne College, Eastbourne

I Have A Dream

I have a dream that all people will be equal,
So black children can go to school.
I have a dream that everyone will be equal,
So no one will be bullied.
I have a dream that people will treat everyone with respect,
So no one will feel alone.
I have a dream that the world will have peace,
Do you?

Olivia Williams (12)
Herbert Shiner School, Petworth

I Have A Dream

I have a dream.

A dream where world hunger is non-existent
M eaning that everyone has what they need.

W here nobody bears any bad qualities, such as
A nger, jealousy and greed.
I have a dream
T hat the guns will fall silent.
I have a dream that the wars will end,
N obody will want to attack anyone.
G uys can just support themselves, each other and fend.

F ights will be known only in story books,
O verall, I dream of a world where
R acism is no more,

T he world wouldn't even care.
H appiness would travel the world
E ndlessly, spreading its joy.

I have a dream,
N obody would steal, whether you're girl or boy.
J obs would go to everyone equally, black or white.
U topia, the only word for it, *a Utopian society!*
S trike down the wicked, smite, smite, smite!
T o end disability, disease and drugs.
I have a dream,
C an it be real?
E ven if it is just a dream.

T ogether, try and make my dream come true.
O verall, put the mistakes of the past behind us.

E verything will always, probably be just a dream.
N o. We will not live in a dream world,
D reams. They can become reality, you know . . .

Rhys Turner (13)
Herbert Shiner School, Petworth

I Have A Dream

I have a dream
To free up the entire world,
To save our lives.

I have a dream
To create a world full of love,
All round, sound, peace.

I have a dream,
Where we're all treated equally,
Where love is free.

I have a dream,
Where everyone talks honestly,
Cut back on lies!

I have a dream.
A safe, calm, relaxed atmosphere,
Where truth runs free.

I have a dream,
Where violence is put to rest,
Fun never sleeps.

Kelly Scutt (12)
Herbert Shiner School, Petworth

I Have A Dream

I dream of a world where starvation is merely a whisper,
Where crimes exist only in films,
Where disease is a dried up lake
And pollution is an empty street.

I dream of a world where war is a deflated balloon,
Where friendship is like a growing tree, blossoming every day,
Where world peace is as constant as the tide
And happiness is an exploding cloud.

Sophie McKenzie (12)
Millais School, Horsham

I Have A Dream

Think of a pebble dropped in a lake,
Of which creates a ripple,
Then another,
Then another,
And another.
Imagine you are the pebble that can create such a huge change
In such a big lake,
All you need is the courage to plunge into the depths
And make that difference.

You are looking out your window,
And see a black cloud, meaning rain,
Do you think about the white cloud, hear that inside
Is the same,
No.
You think of the black cloud being different from the white cloud,
What about you being the black cloud,
Your colour may be different,
But you,
Are the same.

A few raindrops on your window, shall be wiped away,
But when more come and you feel you're getting nowhere,
You give up.
The dream where no one gives in may seem impossible,
But it takes courage and faith to live out that dream.
Don't give up,
Live your dreams.

Jessica Woodall (11)
Millais School, Horsham

A Shrine That's Mine

If I close my eyes I can see it,
My own special place in this life.
No poverty, hunger or suffering,
No weapons or one single knife.

This is my dream and inside it,
Many birds chatter noisily to each other
And children who have been separated,
Will be reunited with fathers and mothers.

My vision is of an ancient shrine,
Where the rusty gate swings in the breeze.
If you close your eyes you can hear it,
The whispering of the trees.

The whole place has a musty smell,
That of incense burnt long ago.
The person who burnt it,
Who am I to know.

A vase of flowers stands on a table,
Dry and crispy, long time dead.
Once in full bloom,
Pink, purple and also red.

A simple oil lamp hangs from the ceiling,
By a twisting blackened chain.
This wonderful building has stood here,
Through wind, sun, snow and rain.

So now if you close your eyes you can see it,
Your own special place in this life,
No poverty, hunger or suffering,
No weapons or one single knife.

Katie Bashford (12)
Millais School, Horsham

I Have A Dream

What's your dream?
Is it to have more money,
To have a bigger house,
Maybe a TV?

My dream,
My hope,
My wish
Is just to stop racism,
Just one thing would make the world a better place,
People are equal
And should be treated with respect,
People should stand up,
Speak up for themselves.

I wish,
I think,
I hope,
Lives,
Innocent lives,
Won't disappear without anyone noticing,
They shouldn't disappear,
They don't disappear,
Not in my dream,
My wish,
My mind.

Lisa Westerdijk (12)
Millais School, Horsham

I Have A Dream - How Can One Dream Change The World?

There are no melting ice caps
No homeless polar bears

No more pollution
No greenhouse gases, too

No more rising of the oceans
No land devoured by the sea

No more cutting down millions upon millions of trees
No more warming of the globe

No more punching holes in the ozone layer
No more destroying our planet

No more Third World, no poverty
No more thirst or starvation

No more child abuse
No more animal fur coats on people

No more smoking - a worldwide ban
No more is the injustice of racism

No more animal cruelty
No more hunting, or extinction

No more, no more, no more:

Just peace.

Aimée O'Callaghan (13)
Millais School, Horsham

I Dreamed A Dream

The headlines say famine has struck,
Thousands at risk, what awful luck.

But I dreamed a dream, I hoped and wished,
That those starving people will all be fed.

The headlines say terrorist bombs kill and maim,
I fear this world has gone insane.

But I dreamed a dream, I hoped and prayed,
That all this killing will soon be stayed.

The headlines say violent crime on the street,
Perhaps you're at risk from everyone you meet.

But I dreamed a dream, that all this would cease,
That the whole of mankind would live in peace.

Alicia Smith (13)
Millais School, Horsham

If I Had A Wish

If I had a wish,
I would let there be peace between nations, leaders,
Friends, families and everyday people.
If I had a wish,
There would be no judgement between what colour,
What you look like or how you talk.
If I had a wish,
Every child would have a loving family, an education
And food and water.
If I had a wish,
No one would suffer death and AIDS
And cancer would cease.
If I had a wish,
In the years to come my wishes would come true.

Caitlin Murray (12)
Millais School, Horsham

I Have A Dream

I have a dream that one day there will be no violence
And people will sort out their differences humanely.

I have a dream that one day soon there will be fairness
Towards all faiths, gender, skin colour and nationalities.

I have a dream that one day there will be no murders, rapes, abuse
Or hatred and that people will be fair, kind and respectful to all.

I have a dream that people won't harm themselves, take drugs
Or commit suicide; instead everyone is happy with themselves
And their lives.

I have a dream that there will be no more stealing, no more greed
And no more break-ins and that people will be happy with what
They have got.

Prue Nash (12)
Millais School, Horsham

I Have A Dream . . .

I have a dream that some day poverty will become extinct . . .
That all the wealth will be equally shared throughout the world.
I have a dream to get a degree and graduate with flying colours . . .
To own a pink Mini and to drive my family around everywhere.
I have a dream that there's plenty of water for everyone . . .
Plus, that technology is cheaper than an elastic band.
I have a dream that disasters will never happen - natural or
                                                    otherwise . . .
For education to be available to the people who need it the most.
I have a dream to cure all illnesses, from a simple cold to a non-
                                                    curable cancer . . .
Hope for no crime, no murder, no droughts and no hunger.
I have a dream, do you?

Ashna Hurynag (13)
Millais School, Horsham

I Had A Dream

As soon as my head sank into my pillow,
I dreamt of all the happiness in the world
And of the bad times that the world has been through in the past.

Why can't people just get along?
Get rid of these debates between countries
That they hate, or don't they care?

As I wandered deeper into my sleep,
I then dreamt of the good times
People have gone through in the past,
Like going out with friends
And going to parties together.

Whenever you look, you *can* see that
Most people *are* having a good time!
But why don't these times last?
The bad times just stick to you like
Super glue, I wish they would shrink away!

Mary-Anne Frank (14)
Millais School, Horsham

My Dream

I believe that justice will be served
I believe that world peace will prevail
I believe that the hungry will get fed
I believe the sick will get better
I believe, I believe
I believe that cruelty to animals will stop
I believe serial killers will stop
I believe child abusers will stop
I believe, I believe
I believe in a smile
I believe in laughter
I believe the world is perfect
I believe in my dream
I believe, I believe.

Jamie Cholwich (14)
Millais School, Horsham

I Have A Dream

I have a dream,
A dream of world peace,
No fighting and no war,
A dream of no starvation,
Food for everyone,
A dream of no abandoned animals,
All safe with loving owners,
A dream of no pollution,
But cars are driving round.

I have a dream,
A dream of no disease,
A cure for every illness,
No droughts,
So no one has to go without water,
A dream of no poverty,
And everyone has money,
A dream of happiness,
Where everyone is equal.

Rebecca Middleton Jones (13)
Millais School, Horsham

I Have A Dream

I have a dream that everyone will be happy,
That the hate in the world will go,
That people will know the truth,
That love will be made in this world of hate,
The storm of anger will clear to make a sunny sky of hope,
The world will be at peace,
No hunger, no poverty, no murders over colour, religion or items,
No disease to spread like wildflowers,
No abandoned animals, hurt and beat,
Only happiness, love and peace.

Hollie Squires (13)
Millais School, Horsham

My Dream

If I close my eyes
What do I see?
Something warm, inviting in front of me.
This place is amazing, fantastic,
Great, happy, ecstatic.

Look up at the sky, it's so clear,
There's only good emotions, no anger, hurt or fear.
Adults are sitting there talking
While children are running and walking,
All having fun
Under the shining sun.

The night is safe, lit by the stars,
There's no criminals behind bars.

All animals are safe,
They are treated with love,
Just like the ozone layer, above.

There's different coloured flowers,
Vibrant in a pretty bed,
But some grow wild in forest and woods,
Free to do as they please just as animals should,
There hasn't been any in cages
For ages and ages and ages,
This is a really wonderful world.

Everyone is healthy,
There are lots of fruit trees,
People eat the fruit sitting in the breeze.

This is my dream, my own special place,
Hopefully it will never change,
Even though life moves on,
This will always be my special space.

Leah Williams (12)
Millais School, Horsham

I Have A Dream

I'm dreaming of a world where everyone is equal.

Why do we treat people differently?
Is it because they're richer or poorer?
Is it because they have different religious beliefs?

I'm dreaming of a world where everyone has a home.

Why can't everyone have a place to live?
Why is it that wealthy people have more than one?
Why does it lead to people begging on the streets?

I'm dreaming of a world where everyone has enough to eat?

Why is it so different, some have plenty, some have none?
I'm dreaming of a place where everyone, richer or poorer
Has the right to live.

This is my dream of a perfect world.

Amy Odell (12)
Millais School, Horsham

My Dream

Each day I read the magazines
And think about the things I've seen,
My friends are entering the events in the papers . . .
This is my dream and I want to enter!
I stand in line to cheer my friends on . . .
One day it will be me and I'll say . . . 'I've won!'
Hicksted, the show you wait and see,
'I'll be there one day and you will be cheering me!'

Lauren Barlow (13)
Millais School, Horsham

I Have A Dream

I have a dream
To wake up in another place,
Another time,
Another world,
Maybe.

I have a dream
To teach a world another life,
Another word,
Another dream,
Maybe.

I have a dream,
To change a life another way,
Another time,
Another mind,
Maybe.

But now on Earth
I'll stay the same,
And hope a dream,
Maybe,
It will be.

I have a dream,
That is certain,
Maybe.

Naomi Hawthorn (13)
Millais School, Horsham

One Day I Wish

One day I wish
That all the
World will treat
Each other equally.

One day I hope
That people will
Work together
To stamp out the
Hatred and cruelty
Of racism.

One day I wish
The dreadful
Misery of poverty
Will dissolve and disappear.

I hope that together
The world will unite
As one and work together
To help stop the
Suffering of the
World's people.

That's what I
Wish to see,
Can you help me?

Olivia Catchpole (12)
Millais School, Horsham

Imagine A Place Far, Far Away

Imagine a place far, far away where there is nothing but sun,
sand and sea.
Imagine just resting under the shade of a tall swaying palm tree.
I touch the soft white sand,
Peace flows all through the land.
My feet are splashing in the glistening sea,
What a wonderful place to be.

Imagine a place far, far away where you can explore leafy jungles
all through the day.
Imagine meeting pandas and tigers running free with room to play.
I hear peaceful silence all around,
Birds are tweeting that's the only sound.
I hear a splashing waterfall,
Not a bad place in the land at all.

Imagine a place far, far away where there are juicy fruits and berries,
Imagine tasting lots of plump red yummy cherries.
I can see tropical birds from the wild,
Singing sweet little tunes that are meek and mild.
Perhaps this island home's not bad at all,
This place is simply wonderful.

Imagine a place far, far away,
I will go home tomorrow, not today.

Elizabeth Hillier (12)
Millais School, Horsham

Take A Look Around

Take a look around,
The world is at rest.
No wars, no fights, no bombs or shouting.
People working together to make the world a better place.

Take a look around,
Everyone is being heard, having his or her say,
Not being judged for what they are on the outside,
But who they are on the inside.
Being chosen last because of how you might act
Is a thing of the past.

Take a look around, in the eyes of another,
Being loved in a proper family surrounded by the most
Positive of things such as constant food and water,
As well as being treated equally,
A dream come true.

Take a look around, how do you want it to be?
A world with a cure for every disease?
A world with a home for everyone and everything?
A world with no starving people
And ever-spreading happiness?
These are the things it could be and should be.

Niamh O'Riordan (12)
Millais School, Horsham

Imagine

Close your eyes - imagine . . .
I close my eyes,
Then open them again,
I see an island so far away,
I start to run towards it,
It seems to be so far, far away,
But finally I reach it.

I keep imagining,

There's nobody there,
It's so peaceful,
The ripples in the sea sparkle,
While the sun in the sky glows.

I keep imagining,

Then out of the blue,
All of a sudden,
A head pokes out.
What can it be?
It's a head of a tiger, I feel alarmed.

I keep imagining,

It comes towards me softly purring,
It gives me a paw,
I take it, delighted,
Then a few more animals come out,
Giraffes, lions, even chimpanzees,

I keep imagining,

But then they fade,
Dreams can come true, but not always.

Roanna Liu (11)
Millais School, Horsham

I Have A Dream

I have a dream
To look up at the stars,
To look up at the stars
And know I made a difference,
However small, however insignificant
To change a life,
To save a life.

I have a dream
To be among the stars,
To be among the stars
And take the pain away,
However small, however insignificant
To start a life,
To take a life.

I have a dream
To see stars die,
To see stars die
And know I helped the world
However small, however insignificant
To watch a life,
To see it soar.

And perhaps, a long time from now,
Before my time is done
Someone will think of me and smile
And I will know
Deep in my heart
That I made a difference,
That I took the pain away,
That I helped the world
And I was among the stars.

Alice Barber (13)
Millais School, Horsham

We Have A Dream - Words Can Change The World

We share a dream that . . .
All people should be treated fairly,
Bullying shouldn't exist
And racism shouldn't be tolerated.
We believe that this dream can come true
And so should you.

We share a dream that . . .
All religious beliefs are respected,
Even if they are not shared,
And everyone's allowed their say.
We believe that this dream can come true
And so should you.

We share a dream that . . .
Peace and happiness will spread around the world,
The rich will support the poor
And children shall not die form thirst or hunger.
We believe that this dream can come true
And so should you.

We share a dream that . . .
No one will be homeless,
Money will not be wasted when it could go to good causes,
Resources should be shared and debt written off.
We believe that this dream can come true
And so should you.

We share a dream that . . .
People will recycle all rubbish,
And we will all work together
To conserve the world's environment,
Safeguarding our planet for the future.
We believe that this dream can come true
And so should you.

We share dreams of a changed world;
We believe that these dreams will come true
When people everywhere unite with one goal:
To make this world a safer, fairer, happier place.

Lucy & Izzy Wood (12)
Millais School, Horsham

Why Do We?

I believe a girl has a right to wear blue,
When everyone else wears pink.
She can play football, cricket and rugby,
All you have to do is think.

Why do we have to be clones
Copying each other's style?
Having the same hair and clothes,
Carrying a nail file.

Why can't we be our own individuals,
Or don't you find that cool?
Why do we waddle around in our heels
Acting like a silly fool?

Why do we get bullied and teased,
For having our own ideas?
Everyone pointing and laughing,
She runs away wiping a tear.

Why do we hide behind an image,
And not stand up for our rights?
We have to believe in our souls,
With a great nation in our sights.

Emmi Edwards (13)
Millais School, Horsham

Heaven's Dream Place

I picture a picture,
Of my dream place,
With sunlight dappling,
Like Heaven's silky lace.

There's a river running halfway through,
I have to believe this place is true.
Wonderful trees standing proud and tall,
Gaps in hedges, through I now crawl.

I picture a picture.

And up a tree, my secret stash,
Of awesome treasures you can't buy with cash.
Sweet blackberries in amongst the heather,
Oh! Nothing can stop the peaceful weather.

I picture the picture.

Cool breeze on my face, gentle and calm,
Earthly smells and wonders rest in my palm.
Here in this place it feels like a blessing,
My version of Heaven - it can't feel depressing.

Who pictures the picture?

Nothing else stands beside me,
Except all of nationality.
Nothing evil in this place,
Just us, a united race.

Let's picture together.

Let's picture a picture,
Of our dream place,
With sunlight dappling,
Like Heaven's silky lace.

Heaven pictures . . .

Katy Brown (11)
Millais School, Horsham

I Have A Dream

I have a dream,
As selfish as it may seem,
To have children without disabilities,
For there to be no wars overseas.

I have a dream,
As selfish as it may seem,
Wish everyone to be equal,
To have a swimming pool full of treacle.

I have a dream,
As selfish as it may seem,
To become a popular actress,
For everyone to sleep on at least a mattress.

I have a dream,
As selfish as it may seem,
For nobody to be poor,
Will this happen? I'm not sure.

April Miller (12)
Millais School, Horsham

I Have A Dream

I dream of a place where you can bounce all day long,
Just swinging and playing and singing a song.
It's a place where no harm can come to you there,
It's a place where everyone really does care.
With a vault, some bars, lots of beams and a floor,
It will keep me happy for evermore.
A way to stay healthy and also have fun,
A place that's far, far away from a gun.
Running and jumping, then away you go,
Up into the air and gone forever, you know.

Laura Hollobon (11)
Millais School, Horsham

To Lose A Friend

Many people will walk in and out of your life,
But only true friends will leave footprints in your heart and soul,
While they have been gone, a part of you is lost,
You take the friendship for granted and then you pay the cost,
You forget how much they mean to you until they go away,
The thought of them being sick haunts you every day,
Life is too short, you don't want to waste even a minute,
You try to enjoy every day and everyone in it,
Tomorrow will come, it could be their last,
You make the most of today, life passes too fast,
You then make a vow to them, to keep until the end,
To keep them through the pain and tears and help their heart mend,
Life is hard, life is tough,
You need to be strong and never give up,
My friend has cancer and soon will die,
I won't give up on her, I will always try,
I can make a difference, I can try my best,
I just think of those who have gone to rest!

Beth Wrigley (14)
Millais School, Horsham

I Have A Dream

I have a dream,
That there is no racism
And that black people are treated the same as white.

I have a dream,
That all poverty will end
And children will not starve on the street.

I have a dream,
That all wars will end, no explosive bombs
Or killing armies anymore.

I have a dream, do you?

Catherine Richardson (12)
Millais School, Horsham

I Have Dreamt A Dream!

I have dreamt a dream,
Where no man did kill,
Animals run around freely,
Doing nothing against their own will.

I have dreamt a dream,
There was peace in the air,
White hands in black,
Walking without a care.

I have dreamt a dream,
Of a beautiful place,
A place full of happiness,
No one without a smile on their face.

I have dreamt a dream,
Of a winter's tale,
Snowy scenes everywhere,
A world where global warming will fail.

I have dreamt a dream,
Where all dreams are mysteries with only one clue,
A mystery yet to be solved,
But please always remember, dreams do come true!

Emma Hollingworth (11)
Millais School, Horsham

We Can Change This World

Close your eyes,
What do you see?
In my eyes,
There is lots of fun for you and me!
A whole theme park made out of choc!
It got built up,
Block by block.

Close your eyes,
What do you see?
A candy rainbow
Above the beautiful sea!
Amazing colours,
Red, yellow, green, blue
Orange and violet,
It looks delicious, I'll have to try it.

Look around you,
What do you see?
A world that can only be fixed
By the help of you and me.
Endangered animals,
It just isn't right,
Unsafe children
Walking around in the night.
We can help it
If we work as a team,
It will save each child, from a scream.

Xanthe Wilson (11)
Millais School, Horsham

I Have A Dream

I think it's important in life,
To always share our views,
Undo the division from black and white
And keep the old and new.

I have a dream about becoming the world's
Most amazing author,
But I also had a dream
About something much longer . . .

I dreamt that I could
Stop world poverty,
End the wars,
That destroy humanity.

Give people their rights
And others, their freedom,
Give all those lost,
Their own little kingdom.

Be nice to the old
And caring to the young
And be loving to those
That have become.

But I am just
An 11-year-old girl,
But some day I wish,
To please the world.

Abigail Joanne Russell (11)
Millais School, Horsham

I Have A Dream

I have a dream,
A dream like no other.
A stop to poverty,
A stop to bullies.

I have a dream,
To create a new world,
Full of people,
A lively swirl.

I have a dream,
Every frown turned
To a merry world,
Where wrongs are learned.

I have a dream,
An ambition to achieve,
Each new creature to turn a new leaf.

I have a dream,
Where hunting has ended,
The creatures unafraid,
Every heart mended.

I have a dream,
To stop and shake hands,
A mission to be
The greatest girl on land.

I have a dream,
A pure desire
To accomplish this task,
As one together.

Betty Cheng (11)
Millais School, Horsham

Imagine

Imagine a place,
A place so beautiful it's unbelievable,
It's my dream place.

There's such a perfect sky, endless and blue
And the sand below me, soft and warm,
It's my dream place.

There's glinting shells, oddly scattered,
Beautiful palm trees swaying,
It's my dream place.

There's even a lagoon,
Clear, warm and calm,
It's my dream place.

The water ripples
So peacefully,
It's my dream place.

I take a walk,
It's so beautiful,
It's my dream place.

Lucy Ansell (11)
Millais School, Horsham

I Have A Dream

I have a dream
To have no more fights
Against the black and whites,
I have a dream
To stop animal cruelty
And to have friends that give loyalty,
I have a dream
For no more rejection
And a world of affection!
Will this dream come true?
Well, that's all up to you.

Kathryn Young (13)
Millais School, Horsham

Forgive You

Maybe I don't want your tears
Your taunts
Your juvenile jaunts
Your hate.

Your eye sets mine running
Your face sets mine blushing
I'm suppressed into silence -
It's emotional violence
It must stop.

Why do you pick me?
The flicker of flame in your eye tells me what,
But not why.
The disdainful glance as I move out of your way
Makes fear bubble in my chest
Like custard that's been left in the microwave.
How can such hatred blossom
From nothing?
I never planted this seed.

So I won't grow it.
You can't blame me
If you were too stoned to do your homework.
You can't blame me
For wanting to get a good grade.

Some day you will know that it's no one's life but your own
And you're wrecking your chances.
Some day you'll feel remorse for kicking me down
As the kid who wore glasses.
Some day you'll hear about me,
But you won't be able to touch me
And that's my dream.

Lindsay Oldham (15)
Millais School, Horsham

I Have A Dream!

I have a dream. It's a dream of a place where I can see
tall green trees that sway in the wind.
I can see animals of all kinds roaming the streets,
the aqua sea and a flowing chocolate waterfall.

In my dream I can hear dodos singing in the trees.
I can hear the waves crashing on the shore
and friends spreading gossip like wildfire.
I feel in this dream, happy and calm,
peaceful, relaxed, secure and safe.

In my dream their knowledge has
brought them a cure and vaccine for AIDS.
I touch the soft golden sand between my toes.
I feel the waves lapping at my feet and the wind ruffling my hair.
I can smell the saltwater, the food cooking on the stove
and the petals of exotic plants. It's a magic place here.

In my dream I can taste the seawater on my tongue,
the rare buffalo meat lavishly cooked and the stewed guar guar fruit.
I have a dream. It's a dream of a place.
That was my dream.

Gloria Singleton (12)
Millais School, Horsham

I Have A Dream

I have a dream that all bullies stayed away,
No one would be scared,
No one would be afraid,
Nobody would cry like somebody just died,
Not even have the courage to close their eyes at night.
I have a dream that all bullies stayed away.
People would be much happier,
They could laugh, chat and even go out to play.

Naomi McMillan (13)
Millais School, Horsham

I Have A Dream

I have a dream
And in this dream I see an angry face
It's the angry face of a man
He is a drunken man
He's staring down at a woman lying on the floor, bleeding

I have a dream
And in this dream I see the woman in a hospital
She is on life support
The angry man next to her is holding her hand
He said she fell down the stairs

I have a dream
That the woman is home
Her husband is hitting her again
She plucks up the courage to call the police
They put him in a cell

I have a dream
That women can be free from their husbands' fists
And that they can get help if they are being hurt
My dream is to stop anger
That is my dream.

Danielle Lindfield (13)
Millais School, Horsham

I Have A Dream

Close your eyes and come with me,
Together we will go and see,
An eco-friendly Earth,
Quiet and calm as peace should be.

No more cars that look like beasts,
Bikes shining on the street.

Birds singing in the air,
Children laughing everywhere.

Happy and relaxed is what you'll feel,
You may even want to do a cartwheel.

Long, green grass that swishes so fast,
The soft leaves fall slowly to the ground.

The fresh air smells as good as chocolate,
Animal scents float around.

Taste the fresh air on your lips,
Tasteful and crisp.

This is my wish,
Yes, this is my wish.

Charlotte Kohn (11)
Millais School, Horsham

I Have A Dream . . .

In my mind,
I have a vision,
A dream of a place,
As perfect as paradise,
Endless white shores,
Clear blue oceans,
Palm trees sway,
In all the commotion!

In my mind,
I have a vision,
A dream of a place,
As perfect as Heaven,
A foaming waterfall,
A refreshing breeze,
Partying people,
I feel at ease.

In my mind,
I have a vision,
A dream of a place
In perfect harmony.
Wild crowds,
Vibrant beasts,
Free horses,
Galloping feet.

A place in a daydream,
A place in my mind,
It is a dream,
It is mine!

Emma Smith (12)
Millais School, Horsham

Dream

One dream, one wish.
A sunny, hot day,
Sparkling waters
And clear skies.
Laughter fills the air,
You can be relaxed,
Free, excited!
If only . . .

One dream, one wish.
Everyone around you,
Playing, singing.
Tall palm trees,
Swaying in the wind.
All us girls can walk free,
Freedom and equality.
If only . . .

One dream, one wish.
Eating all my favourite food,
Not conscious of how I look.
Away from all my problems,
No one will be treated as a slave.
A place full of people.
People to love and care for.
If only . . .

Priya Khosla (11)
Millais School, Horsham

Imagine A World

Imagine a world with no colour,
Imagine a world with no sea,
Imagine a world full of wars,
Imagine what that would be like!

Imagine a world with no wildlife,
Imagine a world with no friends,
Imagine a world with no sound,
That would not be my dream place!

Imagine a world full of colour,
Imagine a world with all round peace,
Imagine a world full of love,
Imagine what that would be like!

Imagine a world with a waterfall full of hope and peace,
Imagine a world where everyone is equal, and no one is judged,
Imagine a world with free wildlife,
That would be my dream place!

Francesca Lodge (12)
Millais School, Horsham

I Have A Dream . . .

I have a dream that people will be judged by their characteristics,
Not by what they look like.

I have a dream that the world will finish having wars,
And make the world peaceful.

I have a dream that people will understand different religions
And stop being racist.

I have a dream that there will be no cruelty to animals,
And that they will be let free.

That is my dream for today!

Ashleigh Jones (13)
Millais School, Horsham

I Have A Dream

I have a dream of comfort,
I have a dream of peace,
I have an idea of what to do
But no one will listen because I'm just a kid.

I have a dream of happiness,
I have a dream of care,
And I have an even better idea of what to do,
But no one will listen because I'm just a kid.

I have a dream of fairness,
I have a dream of rights,
I have a certain idea of what to do,
But no one will listen because if my idea works,
Then they can't say, 'You're just a kid.'

Will anyone listen?

Nicole Barnes (12)
Millais School, Horsham

My Dream

My dream, if I could have it my way,
Would be to listen to what others have to say.

My dream, if I could have it my way,
Would be to help people in every single way.

My dream, if I could have it my way,
Would be to help the willing and stop the killing.

My dream, if I could have it my way,
Would be to praise the Lord and ban the sword.

My dream, if I could have it my way,
Would be to help my brothers and all the others.

Zoë Hassall (11)
Millais School, Horsham

I See The World

I see the world as a better place,
The way God designed it to be,
Shimmering like icing on a cake,
No icebergs cascading into the sea.

I see the world as a better place,
The way God designed it to be,
Factories are a thing of the past,
They won't be troubling me.

I see the world as a better place,
The way God designed it to be,
The smell of freshly fallen snow,
Making the world ever more pretty.

I see the world as a better place,
The way God designed it to be,
No wasted fuel or paper,
Stolen from the humble tree.

I see the world as a better place,
The way God designed it to be,
The sound of tiny animals,
Their distant calls are lively.

I see the world as a better place,
The way God designed it to be,
A perfect immense cloudless sky,
Not polluted by the traitor - a city.

I see the world as a better place,
The way God designed it to be,
I feel waves of exhilaration,
Flowing gracefully over me.

I see the world as a tranquil place,
A place to *live forever, and ever and ever.*

Rosie Inman (12)
Millais School, Horsham

Imagine

Imagine
Imagine a world with no boundaries
No rules and no racism
A world where people can be free
Where people aren't judged for what they look like
But for who they are inside
A world where people can be free

Imagine
Imagine a world with no war
No weapons and no murder
Where people feel safe as they walk
Along the streets late at night in the dark
A world where people can be free
A place where nobody gets drunk
A world with no violence only peace
A world where people can be free

Imagine
Imagine everybody living in safety
Living in harmony and fairness
Everybody being themselves
And feeling good about what they look like
A world where people can be free
Where there is no prejudice or crime
No limits to who you can become
A world where people can be free

Just imagine
Imagine a world like that.

Emily Roche (11)
Millais School, Horsham

I Have A Dream

My dream is to be a chef,
To cook and serve all the guests.

My dream is to be a nurse,
To help a patient to give birth.

My dream is to jump off a plane,
Fly and dive from the sky.

My dream is to fly around the world,
Visit the sights and see celebrities in the spotlight.

My dream is to raise lots of money,
For Comic Relief because it's quite funny.

My dream is to swim with sharks,
For a lark.

My dream is to be a wife,
To give my children a happy life.

My dream is to ride in a hot air balloon,
See the sights and see the views.

My dream is to go skiing
And go fleeing down a hill.

My dream is to climb Mount Everest
Because it's the best.

My dream is to . . . live the dream.

Megan Chinery (13)
Millais School, Horsham

My Dream Is . . .

My dream is . . .
To stop the bullying in the schools
The hitting, the beating, it's all so cruel
The poor child he's frightened, why won't they go?
He eats his lunch sat all alone

My dream is . . .
To help nervous children who want to go to school
Stop the bullies trying to be cool
But there must be a reason behind all of this
Perhaps at home the bully's been dissed

My dream is . . .
For everyone to be accepted
Like we are all expected
Black skin, white skin, nobody's the same
People bully like it's some kind of game
I keep my eyes tightly closed and carry on my dream
No school students at all
None being mean
And as for the victims, they will feel safe with friends
I have finished my dream, it has come to an end.

Alice Bennett (11)
Millais School, Horsham

I Have A Dream

I have a dream
To change the world,
To have no wars,
To obey all laws.

I have a dream
Of a healthy world.
I have a dream
Of a wealthy world,
To get rid of litter
And to all be fitter.

I have a dream
Of black and white,
Not to fight
But to be alike.
I have a dream
Of world peace,
To form a human alliance.

I have a dream
To help the poor
And give them a lot more.
I have a dream
That needs to come true
And not reform World War II.
When I wake, I hope to make
This world we live in a better place.

Jade Hill (13)
Millais School, Horsham

I Have A Dream

I have a dream.
I dream of no crime.
No more suffering,
Much more caring.
I dream of peace,
Peace all over Earth.
More friendliness,
Less anger,
Happiness complete.
Happiness complete.

I have a dream.
I dream of no wars.
No more weapons,
Much more love.
I dream of peace,
Peace all over Earth.
More generosity,
Less poverty,
Perfectness complete.
Perfectness complete.

Rebecca Eglinton (12)
Millais School, Horsham

I Have A Dream!

I have a dream
To live in peace,
No racism or wars,
To unite as one
And not to single out others
For having their own opinion,
To cut down on pollution,
Drugs and abuse.
This is my dream,
Come and share it!

Lauren Cole (12)
Millais School, Horsham

I Have A Dream

I have a dream
To make the world a better place,
To put a smile on that poor, unhappy face.
I have a dream
To stop animal cruelty in every single way,
I have a dream and I'm going to have a say.
To watch these animals go through pain and suffer,
For what? For nothing, I want them to get tougher.
I want the people to see and feel what most animals go through,
And let people know they're hurting too.
If you can feel what I can, animal cruelty should be no longer,
Then stand up tall and let your heart grow stronger.
We are strong as people every day,
Animals are always there for you in every way,
So give something back to the loyal animal kind,
They deserve it like we deserve our freedom.
Hunting and killing is no fun and certainly not cool,
Because whoever does it is a certain fool.
So stop it now before it's too late,
This is not any animal's fate.
Please help me, help these amazing creatures,
They shouldn't be a part of a fur coat's features.
So listen up, listen good because *I have a dream*
And it deserves to be heard and made reality.

I may not be the great Luther King,
But he showed us all if you don't give up
And fight for what you believe in,
Your dream could become reality
For the greater good of man and even animal kind
And that's what I intend to do.

Shannon Tate (13)
Millais School, Horsham

One Day

One day, the world will be united,
No one will be isolated or afraid.
Black and white people will stand together,
Cruelty and danger will be put to rest.

One day, the world will be happy,
No one will wear long gloomy faces,
Wars will come to an immediate halt,
Because there will be peace and freedom forever.

One day, all crimes will be stopped,
The ice caps refrozen and intact.
Life as we know it will get better and better,
No harm or danger will come.

One day, global warming will have ended,
All illness like cancer will be cured,
Suffering and pain will have disappeared,
Poverty will just be a memory.

One day, people will live as long as they can,
Technology will have expanded,
But everyone will be fit and healthy,
We'll all excel in what we do.

One day, shelter won't be a hardship
And money will be easy to find.
Deaf and blind people will see and hear,
There will be nothing to ever fear.

One day, maybe,
But why not make one day today?

Chloe Fletcher (12)
Millais School, Horsham

I Had A Dream

I had a dream
To stop all bad things,
But then I realised
What could I do,
Just me on my own?
How could I make a difference,
Me in my whirlpool of bad things?

But terrible news
Arrived the next day,
A boy I sponsored
Had just passed away.
He died of disease
And coldness too,
If only I made my dream come true,
If I could save lives
And if I could stand up
Against the world
And lend a hand,
But people keep going
And people do nothing,
So people disappear
From this life cycle ring.

I had a dream
Which I did not follow,
I just sat back
And watched all the sorrow.

So learn from me,
Make something new
And try and make a dream come true!

Alice Bish (11)
Millais School, Horsham

I Have A Dream

I have a dream,
I see a place,
A place of peace,
Like paradise.
The human race,
In harmony,
Have banished fear
And poverty.
I have a dream,
That crime and war,
Have left the Earth,
For evermore.
No more hurting,
No more spite,
Only peace
And always light.

Hannah Jones (12)
Millais School, Horsham

I Have A Dream

I have a dream
For all to be calm,
The world to be a team
And come to no harm.

For no war to come,
The world to be at peace,
For all to learn
To make all war cease.

It may never happen,
It may just be a dream,
But it may come,
Like other things you have seen.

Jade Coates (11)
Millais School, Horsham

I Dream Of A Place

I have a dream,
I see it when I close my eyes,
It's always there at the back of my mind.

I see a place where
Nobody's unhappy,
No one's scared,
Everybody's cheerful
And everyone's prepared.

If you close your eyes
You will see it too,
With all the people,
Their hopes coming true.

It could be more than just amazing,
It could be more than just my dreams coming true,
It could be more than just what I want,
It could be perfect for you too.

Rebecca Pannell (11)
Millais School, Horsham

I Have A Dream

I have a dream where perfection does not exist,
Where everyone can be whatever they want to be
And never be a risk.
I have a dream where there is no danger for anyone to fear
And where all the gangs and terrorists will disappear.
I have a dream where war and famine will end,
And where everyone will have a spare hand to lend.
I have a dream where everyone's wishes will come true.
I have a dream, how about you?

Raffaella Parente (13)
Millais School, Horsham

Imagine A Place

Imagine a world with a warm golden sun,
A place where the waves crash against the shores,
A place you can go to think.

Imagine a world with a purple sunset,
A place where the sand glistens in the sunlight,
A place everyone is relaxed.

Imagine a world with towering palm trees,
A place of rest and happiness,
A place where everything is perfect.

Imagine a world with a gentle warm breeze,
A place where dreams come true,
A place where everyone is equal.

Imagine a world with sparkling waters,
A place with eternal safety,
A place where everyone gets along.

Laura Turnbull (12)
Millais School, Horsham

I Have A Dream To Change The World

I have a dream
That all bullies were gone,
We were all friends
And we all got on.

I have a dream
That there were no fights,
Everyone together,
Black or white.

I have a dream
That all wars will end,
Together as one
We are all friends.

Carol Leonard (12)
Millais School, Horsham

I Have A Dream

I have a dream,
To wake up in the morning and realise that
My childhood dream is now reality.

I have a dream,
That my dreams are not dreams anymore.

I have a dream,
When I have a big house with children
And a husband who is there for me always;

I have a flashy red car and - money, *money, money*
Photographers live outside my door, I am their priceless diamond.
I try to wake up, the realisation is, this is a dream, no more.

I smile, I gasp,
I love the life I'm living
And I live the life I'm loving.
I expect to hear the ring of an alarm bell to wake me up,
But no ringing is heard.
Then I thought to myself, *I put myself here, I made this reality,*
I am proud of who I am and nothing is going to change that.

Amanda Leslie (13)
Millais School, Horsham

I Have A Dream . . .

Imagine a world with no poverty,
What a better place that world would be.

Imagine a world with peace all around,
That's a world that should be found.

Imagine a world with no pollution,
That would be a great solution!

Imagine a world with no rubbish to be seen,
Then that world would be really clean.

Imagine a world with less CO_2,
The hole in the ozone would close up soon.

Imagine a world where no diseases are found,
Then we'd all be safe and sound.

Imagine a world in your head,
Let's hope you'll see it before you're dead.

Louisa Clark (12)
Millais School, Horsham

I Have Wishes

I have wishes,
I wish for the extinction of the litterbug,
I wish for friends among enemies,
I wish for no more diseases,
I wish for peace on a worldwide scale,
I wish for enough food and water for everyone,
I wish for everyone to be equal,
I wish for no more pollution,
I wish for animals never to be homeless,
I wish for all my wishes to come true.
What do you wish for,
And can you make them a reality?

Alysha Elkins-Green (13)
Millais School, Horsham

I Had A Dream . . .

I had a dream . . .
That all the racism would stop one day and the two colours
would become one.
I had a dream . . .
That everyone was seen as equal and the bullying would stop.
I had a dream. . .
That everyone in the world was friends and liked each other.
I had a dream . .
That child abuse ended and the victims could get on with their lives.
I had a dream . . .
That children were happy and safe from violence.
I had a dream. . .
That all cruelty to animals would stop.
I had a dream . . .
That all the terrorists would stop attacking the world.
I had a dream . . .
That all innocent people stopped getting hurt.
I had a dream . . .
That the Iraq war was over.
I had a dream . . .
That everybody was happy being them and in their body.
I had a dream . . .
That all this was only a dream.

Kirsty Towes (14)
Millais School, Horsham

I Have A Dream To Change The World

I have a dream to change the world
Black and white would get along in peace
No more wars over what faith
What race, what colour your skin is

I have a dream to change the world
Poverty and hunger would end
No rich or poor, everyone equal
Money of the world shared happily

I have a dream to change the world
Bullies would stop terrorising dreams
No more kicks, no more punches
No more victims in this world.

Natalie Burgess (12)
Millais School, Horsham

A Dream That Would Change The World

I think we should stop all child abuse,
I don't know why it happens, there is no excuse.

We should get along with everyone,
It doesn't matter if you are black or white,
Everyone has feelings and everyone's right.

We should look out for the people on the street
And look out for everyone that we meet.

We should look out for the homeless and poor,
That's one thing we should do more.

children and even adults get offended,
If we are nice their hearts can be mended.

Kelly Lord (12)
Millais School, Horsham

I Have A Dream

I have a dream of a budding writer,
Everyone would know her name.
I dream of that writer being me, of course,
I dream of being swamped with fame.
I don't want to end up obsolete,
A dull drone to bore the mass,
I want to be bubbly, zany and smart,
With a hint of 'kerpow' and 'pizzazz'!

I have a dream of a world with no animal testing,
A perfectly humane time.
I want to write a book like Black Beauty,
Change a lot of people's minds.
A world without this cruel abuse
Would be a great world indeed,
So that people can appreciate
A knight *and* his great steed.

I have a dream of doing something,
Something important and great,
I know I should probably not jinx it,
I should leave it up to fate.
What I can do is try not to be fazed,
Not to be afraid of being loud,
Because then I might end up
Being just another face in the crowd.

Julia Tansley (11)
Millais School, Horsham

What Is A Dream?

A dream is a wonderful thing,
It floats through your head
Like a butterfly on a long summer's day.
It can come true like a wish,
It can blossom like a tree,
It can shine like a star,
A dream is a wonderful thing.

A dream is a magical thing,
It might be impossible, it might not be.
It might stand strong, it might flicker.
You could search and never find one,
You could search and find hundreds.
A dream is as mysterious as the mist.
A dream is a magical thing.

A dream is a searching thing,
It searches your heart
And it pulls from your heart
The one thing you desire
And it stays in your mind
For the rest of your life.
A dream is a searching thing.

A dream is everlasting.

Abigail Pollard (11)
Millais School, Horsham

I Had A Dream

I had a dream
That the world was at peace.
Peace, peace, peace.
That wars would come to a halt,
Poverty would stop
And racism would be history,
Never to be revisited again.
I had a dream
That there was no more violence.
Violence, violence, violence.
No killing, murders or fights,
Just calm days and calm nights.
I had a dream
That there were no more floods, hurricanes, volcanic eruptions,
Tsunamis, tornadoes
Which destroy people's homes, friends and families.
I had a dream
That bombs stopped dropping.
Dropping, dropping, dropping.
Killing many people, squashing homes, destroying countries.
I had a dream
That famine would come to an end.
I had a dream,
I had a dream.

Jessica Chapman (12)
Millais School, Horsham

I Have A Dream

It starts with a quarrel
And then with a fight
I get so scared
I can't sleep at night

You push me and shove me
You make me fall back
You hit me and punch me
Because my skin's black

I want it to stop
I want to be glad
I wish it would change
It makes me so mad

Oh, why am I bullied?
I really don't know
They say it will change
But this is not so

But I have a dream
And dreams can come true
This world can be better
For me and for you.

Nicola Kennedy (12)
Millais School, Horsham

I Had A Dream . . .

I had a dream of a world just like ours, but better,
Where soft wind blows through forests of untouched trees,
Where nothing is injured by human pride,
The world is bathed in a soft sunlight, not burnt in its mighty rays,
No sound of cars on motorways, no smell of petrol in the breeze,
A horse neighs in the distance, galloping as free as this dreamworld,
A small child runs past, giggling, doing what she pleases,
And behind her a fawn, not afraid of men with guns,
But curious at the wide open space
And the soft blades of grass at his hooves,
A village I come upon, and bright and merry it is,
For they all live in harmony, no bullying, hate or deceit,
There is no law, for no need of one,
As everyone lives how they should,
And soon I realise what a perfect world this is,
But I know it can't be real, for no matter how hard we try
We won't get it right,
So I call out to any who will listen, a plea on a rather large scale,
Don't ruin this world we've got, rescue it, save it, love it . . .

Lucy Croker (11)
Millais School, Horsham

I Have A Dream

I have a dream to be a star
And own a flash car.

I have a dream to rule the world
And be a cool girl.

I have a dream to be a nurse
And not let ill people get any worse.

I have a dream to be a superstar
And go far.

Emma Nias (12)
Millais School, Horsham

I Have A Dream

I have a dream to make a cure for the endless hate,
Killing
And war.

I have a dream, to save the Earth,
The animals,
Creatures, the seas
And birds.

I have a dream to live in peace,
Give people harmony,
Bring destruction to a cease.

I have a dream to let out good,
To end all poverty,
I really should.

I have a dream,
To save a life,
Relive the days where no one stood in strife.

Aimee Azhar (11)
Millais School, Horsham

I Have A Dream

I have a dream every day
That everything will be OK.
I wish, I wish the world would be
A better place for you and me.
The wars would stop, the killing would go,
Imagine a better place for us to grow.
I have a dream that the world would be
A better place for you and me.

Rebecca Williams (14)
Millais School, Horsham

I Had A Dream - To Change The World

I had a dream,
That there were no more bullies,
They had all gone,
I could live life fully.

I had a dream,
That I could walk free,
It was so nice,
To just be me.

I had a dream,
That life was fun,
I didn't worry,
Or lie to my mum.

I had a dream,
There were no more fights,
Or whether people
Were black or white.

Emma Gray (12)
Millais School, Horsham

My Dream

My dream is to stop animal testing,
If it's the last thing I do.
It can make the animals ill
And they can get a disease too.
Think of all the animals,
What have they done to you?
Why do we test on them
Just to make shampoo?

Karly Masters (11)
Millais School, Horsham

I Have A Dream

I have a dream
To stop the bullies and the racists.
Who gives them the right to
Speak foul-mouthed?

But will that dream come true?
Trying to stop the bullies
And what they're putting
The victims through?

I have a dream
To stop the bullies and the racists.
Who gives them the right to
Speak foul-mouthed?

This is a dream I wish for
And maybe if I dream more,
Maybe this dream will happen!
And it will have because I believe

I have a dream.

Sarah Meeking (12)
Millais School, Horsham

I Have A Dream

One day I wished I could end starvation,
But was this wish just my imagination?
One day I wished people could live longer than before.
One day I wished I could end all war.
I thought I saw the end to animal testing,
But these were only dreams from when I was resting.
Dreams become reality, it only takes one dream,
The future is in your hands.

Beth MacDonald (12)
Millais School, Horsham

I Had A Dream

I had a dream,
We live in a world moving faster and faster,
Heard it so often we're bored with disaster.
Governments seem to be losing their grip,
Nowhere to jump from this sinking ship.
The bigger the problem, the smaller we feel,
But things that we do help the planet to heal.

I had a dream that we
Switch off a light to save energy,
Don't fill the kettle to make one cup of tea,
And to recycle the paper, the metal, the glass,
Stops the landfill tips filling up too fast.
Avoid buying objects you don't really need,
Resist the temptation of envy and greed.

I had a dream that in my world there was
No person you bully at school,
No person who doesn't know how to be cool,
No person living alone with these fears,
No person destroyed by his peers,
No person who drowns in your scorn,
No person who wishes he hadn't been born,
No person you destroy for fun,
No person sitting looking glum,
No person whose name you don't know,
No person who can't let go,
No person who doesn't have feeling too,
Just people the same as you!

Make a change to the world.

Demi Mantell (13)
Millais School, Horsham

I Have A Dream!

I hope one day that people will see the world like me,
For I have a dream of a better place.
In my dream, no one litters, it's all clean.
There are no bullies at school, no teaches are mean.
In a world of my own it's all lush and divine,
The hillsides are pretty, everyone is just fine.
Nobody's sad, crying or angry,
There are lots of shops, loads of shops all filled with candy.
Every book is exciting and filled with adventure,
Nature's still there, still as lovely as ever.
No one is dumb, everyone's clever.
Men don't destroy with their machines and their tree-breakers,
The paper's recycled, we live on no wood,
The birds can still nest, oh yes, they should.
No one gets ill or catches the flu,
The animals are safe, the cows still go 'moo'.
No one smokes, no one hits, murders or robs,
Everyone is treated with the same respect,
No one laughs at anyone unless there's a joke,
Everyone has money, nobody gets broke.
I wish everyone could just get along,
No one feels left out, they feel they belong.
Nobody dies unless they're very old,
There's no such thing as cancer, diabetes or a cold.
Oh, if only the world revolved around this,
It would be the best place, a place of great bliss.

Amy Zimmermann (11)
Millais School, Horsham

I Have A Dream

I have a dream . . .
That no one will argue because there will be nothing to argue about.
I have a dream . . .
That trees and rainforests will never be chopped down,
They will stand tall forever.
I have a dream . . .
That cruelty will stop, animals will be able to roam free,
Not be squashed up in cages.
I have a dream . . .
That child abuse, murders and racism will stop,
Everyone will live in peace.
I have a dream . . .
That there is no fighting, war, bombs or enemies.
I have a dream . . .
No one will be ill, there will be a cure for cancer,
Bird flu and diseases.
I have a dream . . .
The world is a place of peace and happiness.
I have a dream . . .
That everything has food to eat, a place to stay
And a doctor to see if needed.
I have a dream . . .
The world is a better place.
I have a dream ...

Heather Dolan (12)
Millais School, Horsham

I Have A Dream

I have a dream that people will get on,
That people will be at peace with each other.

I have a dream that there will be no wars,
That no bombs will fall from the sky.

I have a dream that there is an end to all illness,
That they have help and the medicines they need.

I have a dream that there will be no more starvation,
That people will go to bed with full tummies.

I have a dream that there will be no cruelty to animals,
That animals will be fed and looked after.

I have a dream that homeless people will be off the streets,
That they will have a roof over their heads.

I have a dream that people will get enough clean water
So that animals and crops will grow and live.

I have a dream that people will be paid fairly,
That people in other countries will have more money to live.

I have a dream that there will be no racism,
That people can do what they want, no matter the colour of their skin.

Charlotte Inge (12)
Millais School, Horsham

I Have A Dream

They spit, they shout, they muck about, finding people to annoy,
Then it sticks, never goes away, you feel you'll never find joy.

I have a dream to help this world, stop bullying in every way,
But will it work? I'll never know, I haven't been a victim of this game.

They punch, they kick, they even flick, call names that hit you hard,
But you still cry, you still hurt, the pain cuts you like a shard.

I have a dream to help this world, stop bullying in every way,
But will it work? I'll never know, I haven't been a victim of this game.

They kicked, they flicked, they pinched, they punched,
But that doesn't worry you now.
Those words they said will always stick
But you will never be treated as if you're foul.

I have a dream to help this world, stop bullying in every way,
But will it work? I'll never know, I haven't been a victim of this game.

Amy O'Connor (12)
Millais School, Horsham

I Have A Dream

I have a dream for all the changes in the future,
That all poverty will end.
I have a dream for all the homeless people,
That each and every person will have their own place to be.

I have a dream that one day all people will have
Even a small amount of money,
That there will be no starving.
I have a dream that all wars will stop,
No fighting to the death.

Imagine a world where everyone's happy.
Imagine a world where people are treated equally.
Imagine all the people living life their own way.
Imagine a peaceful world.

Annie Nye (12)
Millais School, Horsham

I Have A Dream

I have a dream that no one dies from cruelty alone,
I have a dream that people in need are never on their own,
I have a dream that I can cure the poverty in this world,
I have a dream that everyone cares, please let them all be told.

Think of a world where all is pain and everyone's alone,
Then think of a world where all is happiness
And nobody's on their own.

I have a dream that everyone's happy and they
Have all that they need,
I have a dream that the rich would give to others,
Instead of just giving themselves a treat.
I have a dream that there is rain for all the crops to grow.
I have a dream that all dry rivers would fill and start to flow.

Think of a world where all is hunger and everybody starves,
Then think of a world where everyone's eating,
Be it a small amount or be it large.

I have a dream that'll change the world,
I have a dream that needs your help to unfold.

Clare Hurst (12)
Millais School, Horsham

I Have A Dream

I have a dream that bombs will not fall,
I have a dream that people will stand tall,
I have a dream that hunger will never happen,
I have a dream that evil we will flatten,
I have a dream that black or white, we will stand together
day and night,
I have a dream that light fills dark places,
I have a dream that I will only see happy faces,
I have a dream that people will eat their fill,
I have a dream that people will no longer kill,
I have a dream . . .

Daisy Keeling (11)
Millais School, Horsham

I Had A Dream

I had a dream last night where I flew to another world,
A place with clear blue skies, no pollution,
A place where the word 'war' didn't exist,
A place where poverty was a thing of the past,
A united place where it didn't matter who you were
Or what you looked like, just that you were human.
It was too perfect to be true.

I had a dream last night where I flew to another world,
The skies were grey, thick with pollution,
A place where the word 'war' was spread over the newspapers
And TV headlines as if it was a routine,
A place where people lay on the streets and were starving to death,
A world where the countries were spread apart, hating and
                                                killing their neighbours.

I had a dream last night where I didn't fly to another world,
I saw the truth as if someone was opening a door.
Our skies are becoming grey,
The word 'war' doesn't have the same effect as it used to,
It's almost becoming the norm.
People are out there, starving on our streets
And the countries are moving slightly apart.
I don't want this world to be perfect,
But I don't want this world to be ruined.
I had three dreams and learnt the truth,
And now it's time to do something!

Victoria Sillett (12)
Millais School, Horsham

I Have A Dream

I have a dream to stop smoking.
I have a dream to stop animals from being hunted.
I have a dream to get better equipment for schools.
I have a dream to stop pollution from destroying
The ozone layer that supplies us with oxygen.
I have a dream to make beaches cleaner.
I have a dream to make parks litter-free.
I have a dream to stop illegal drugs
From being sold on the black market.
I have a dream to treat everyone with fairness and respect.
I have a dream to ban all alcohol and drugs.
I have a dream to make subways more colourful.
I have a dream to make cities cleaner.
I have a dream to stop punks from doing graffiti on buildings.

Safiyah Dinaully (11)
Millais School, Horsham

I Have A Dream That All Poverty Will End

I have a dream that one day all world poverty will end
And all people will live in peace.
I have a dream that one day people will live in harmony
And people will never starve.
I have a dream that one day people will have running water
In their homes, and central heating.
I have a dream that all people will have a good education
And that all people will go to work.
I have a dream that all people can eat.
I have a great dream that the world will be a better place.

Jade Wilkinson (12)
Millais School, Horsham

I Had A Dream

I had a dream, a dream of peace and justice,
An end to war and hatred,
I wanted to smile at the Devil and overrule evil
To make the world a better place.
That was my dream.

I had a dream, a dream of thanks and forgiveness,
A fresh start in life, a new beginning,
I wanted friend to defeat foe,
To make the world more pleasant.
That was my dream.

I had a dream, a dream of courage and bravery,
An end to racism and bullying,
I want everyone to be proud of who they are,
To stand up for themselves, to have their rights.
That was my dream.

And when I look at the world today,
I realise it was only a dream, nothing more.

Lucy Bushell (12)
Millais School, Horsham

I Have A Dream

I have a dream that
Global warming never walk this Earth
And peace roam again once more.

I have a dream that
Separation between parents is no more
And that Africa is showered with rain.

I have a dream that
Loneliness never roam this Earth,
Everyone listen to people again and everyone helps charities.

Hannah Wheatley (11)
Millais School, Horsham

I Have A Dream

I have a dream
That maybe one day
I can say
I have accomplished my dreams.

I have a dream
To own my own café,
Then I can say
I have accomplished my personal dream.

I have a dream
That maybe one day, everyone will be
Treated the same way,
Then I can say
I have accomplished my national dream.

I have a dream
To start world peace,
Then I can scream
I have accomplished my international dream.

Alexandra Bohan (13)
Millais School, Horsham

Global Warming

I have a dream about no global warming,
The end of the cold winters that will soon be dawning,
The polar caps are going,
Pollution is growing,
People don't care,
For penguins it's not fair!
Tides will rise,
Nobody even realises
Pollution is destroying the Earth!

Tessa Smith (13)
Millais School, Horsham

I Have A Dream

I had a dream, yes I did,
About myself.
I want to be a heart surgeon, or a bypass surgeon,
I want to help people get well.

I had a dream, yes I did,
About the world.
I want a better NHS for people,
Free help to the sick, so they don't have to pay.

I had a dream, yes I did,
About myself.
I want to be a rugby player and play for England
And get more people into sports.

I had a dream, yes I did,
About the world.
I want to help children get more active,
I want more sports for children.

Elizabeth Hillman (11)
Millais School, Horsham

I Have A Dream

I have a dream that one day there will be no war,
No countries will have enemies,
No weapons will be used,
No violence when we walk down the street,
No racism, no sadness, no loss,
No one to be afraid of what they're going to see when they turn
the next corner,
I want a world where parents feel safe letting their children go and
Play in the park, without having a doubt they will never return,
I want to feel safe walking down my road,
I want this world to live in peace.
I have a dream and I want it to be heard.

Abbie Jenkins (13)
Millais School, Horsham

I Had A Dream

I had a dream of a better place
Far beyond the sea.
I had a dream of a better place,
Why is it nowhere near me?
I had a dream of a better place
Filled with peaceful sounds.
I had a dream of a better place
Where happiness knew no bounds.
I had a dream of a better place,
Where evil isn't known.
I had a dream of a better place
Where flowers are always grown.
I had a dream of a better place
Where the sun will always shine.
I had a dream of a better place,
I wish it could all be mine.
I had a dream of a better place
Far beyond the sea.
I had a dream of a better place,
Why is it nowhere near me?

Nicola Dyer (12)
Millais School, Horsham

I Have A Dream

I have a dream to cure the world of cancer,
I have a dream to rid the world of murder,
To stop poverty and animal cruelty.
I have a dream to not fear the outside,
I have a dream to feel safe and free,
I have a dream where everyone is treated the same,
No matter what.
I have a dream that one day this will happen.

Katy Rode (13)
Millais School, Horsham

I Have A Dream

I have a dream
For world happiness,
For no more wars,
For no more bombers.

I have a dream
To stop poverty,
To stop animal cruelty,
To stop starvation.

I have a dream
To be safe in the dark,
To be safe in the street,
To be safe in my home.

I have a dream
With no child abuse,
With no bullying,
With no fear.

I have a dream
With no more murders,
With no more abductions,
With no more sadness.

I have a dream
That my name is known,
For the best beauty salon,
Called *'Don't Touch!'*

I have this dream
And someday it will be a reality.

Emma Redgrove (13)
Millais School, Horsham

I Have A Dream

I have a dream that one day the whole world will be at peace.
I wish that one day the word 'poverty' doesn't exist.
I wish people would think about the thousands of people
Dying of famine.

I want people to live over 12,
For them to live life to the full,
For them to have a house of luxury,
And people won't care at all.

I want people to get an education
And get HIV medication.
I want people to have running water,
That's not hard at all.

I want people to be treated fairly,
And not be judged by the colour of their skin.
I want terrorism out of our lives,
I don't want people to fight.

I have a dream that one day the world will be at peace,
I wish that one day the word 'poverty' doesn't exist.
I wish people would think about the thousands of people
Dying of famine.

Catherine Pickett 13)
Millais School, Horsham

I Have A Dream

I have a dream to be a star,
To fly high and go far,
To fly as far as the sky,
For people to idolise me
For being everything they wanna be,
To be in a magazine,
Maybe even be the Queen.

Imogen Hay (13)
Millais School, Horsham

Animal Cruelty

I hear the lion's padding paws,
I hear it give a mighty roar,
What once was bold
Sounds grave and old,
It's anguished to the core.

I see the lion's cuts and sores,
Locked behind closed, barred doors,
Exiled as a circus freak,
Never able to find the life it seeks,
Surely there must be laws.

As it lies down in its den,
Surrendering to the cruel men,
No one is around to weep,
He prepares for the eternal sleep,
Never to wake again.

Every day animals unfairly die,
In Alaska 100 at a time,
Animal cruelty *has* to stop.

Stephanie Moir (12)
Millais School, Horsham

I Have A Dream

I have a dream where the world will be a better place.
Stop the killing, stop the violence and
Stop all the bad things that happen in the world.

I have a dream where all animal testing shall stop
And no animals will be hurt.

I have a dream where I can grow up
And become one of the most famous master chefs around
And have my own restaurant.

These are my dreams, my only dreams and
I hope that one day they will come true.

Miriam Playfoot (12)
Millais School, Horsham

My Dream

I have a dream,
It sings to me,
Inside it makes me feel happy.

To be a musician in New York, somewhere,
To feel the 'buzz' of the city air.

I want to know that the world is clean,
safe, alive, to feel serene.

I want to have been to the extreme,
I want to tell people what I've done,
Where I've been, I want to have fun.

I want my life to have some spice,
I want everyone to hear, even the mice,
About my wishes, my thoughts,
My dream.

Jasmine Hutchings (13)
Millais School, Horsham

I Have A Dream

My dream is for peace for all mankind,
My dream is for no racism, sexism, but kind,
My dream is for no cruelty to animals or kids,
My dream is for peace on Earth
For all who live on it,
My dream is for no criminals to roam the streets,
My dream is for love and hope and peace,
My dream is for happiness for all who wish for it,
My dream is for forgiveness for all who sin,
My dream is for friends to be friends forever,
My dream is for none to suffer the way I did,
My dream is for a better world,
Better than mine.

Elisa Lawrance (12)
Millais School, Horsham

I Have A Dream!

Listen up, my name is Kayleigh
And this is my dream . . .

I feel their pain,
To hear them cry
I think of those who have died,
I wish I could,
I know I will
One day,
Some day,
I will stop the pain.

I'll work and work,
I'll make it happen,
One day,
Some day,
I will stop the pain.

When I am older,
I'll be bolder,
I can make this change,
One day,
Some day,
I will stop the pain.

I'll work,
I'll strive,
I'll help them stay alive,
One day,
Some day.

My dream's to stop this happening,
My dream's to stop the pain,
My dream's to help these animals
Live their lives again.

Kayleigh Fuller (13)
Millais School, Horsham

In This World

I have a dream
That in this world
Animal cruelty will stop.
In this world
There'll be no poverty.
In this world,
Racism will be stopped.
In this world
Everyone will be loved.
In this world
Friendship will never break.
In this world
Children will stop crying in pain.
In this world
Everyone will have enough water.
In this world
There'll be no limits.
In this world
There'll be smiles all round.
I have a dream that
The world will be our world.
I have a dream . . .
The biggest dream of all,
That everyone and everything will be *happy!*

Harriet Lloyd (13)
Millais School, Horsham

I Have A Dream

I have a dream,
My dream is not simple,
My dream does not have to be complex.

Some may say that it is impossible,
Others may say that it is a start,
Then I would say, after all that,
I have accomplished my dream and that is that.

Although my dream will never end
I will stay true right to the end.
My dream may not be your dream,
But it is also my dream to make it your dream.

I will make a solution to stop pollution,
That's how I imagine the world.
I will stop animal cruelty,
That's how I imagine the world.
I will house the homeless and treat the sick,
That's how I imagine the world.
I will make world peace,
That's how I imagine the world.

I have a dream!

Gail Betts (12)
Millais School, Horsham

I Have A Dream!

I have a dream to own a villa,
A villa in Italy, that will make my life better.
I want a cat, maybe two,
A golden retriever will do the job too.
I want a swimming pool
For swimming in the sun,
And having pool parties that will be fun.
I have a dream
To travel the world
And meet new people
Who speak differently to me.
I want to grow up wealthy and healthy,
Get a good job and earn lots of money,
Maybe be on TV,
Or be a model for a new magazine.
As I've grown up my dream has changed,
I first wanted to be a princess,
Live in a palace with my very own servants,
But now to me that's all a joke.
That was my dream, I hope it comes true,
There's bound to be more coming soon.

Daniela Defeo (13)
Millais School, Horsham

I'm That Girl

I'm that girl
That has a dream
That we will work together
As a team.

I'm that girl
That wants to see
Stopping of racism
And poverty.

I'm that girl
That wants to hear
Children playing,
Hiding no fear.

I'm that girl
That wants world peace,
To see the care
And give an increase.

I'm that girl
That hides away,
But when I'm older
I'll do this one day.

Harriette Wysocki (13)
Millais School, Horsham

I Have A Dream . . .

A monkey's life is fun - it's thumping,
Swinging, eating, playing, jumping,
But this is not my life at all,
It's simply not that fun - it's cruel.
My cage is only two feet tall,
I sit huddled - leave me - I plead.
They stab needles and make me bleed,
Spray cans of stuff into my eyes.
At night I get attacked by flies.
In the darkness and cold I sit alone,
Hoping someone shall give me a home
Far away from products I hate,
Perhaps for me it's just too late.
Shampoos and cream, tablets galore,
Even when I'm ill I get more.
I had a dream that this was me,
Stuck in a monkey's misery.
Now I know their awful state,
Better help now before it's too late.
I have a dream . . . of animal freedom.

Zoe Turner (13)
Millais School, Horsham

Full Stop

I have a dream racism would stop.
All the bad things that have happened turn back the clock.
I wish we could take back what forefathers have done.
I cannot really be the only one.
All the pain and suffering it has caused.
No one in their right mind should ever applaud.
It can't be right, it can't be ignored.
They must have been extremely bored.
I can't be the only one of course, who thinks racism
Should end . . . *full stop.*

Tom Pearce (13)
Newlands School, Seaford

Vision

I visualise that children should be happy
And not get bullied at school or at home.
I dream that this will make a better world.

I visualise that the level of crime will drop
And people will feel safer walking in the streets.
I dream that this will make a better world.

I visualise that people will stop smoking
And it will be banned.
I dream that this will make a better world.

I visualise that the streets will be clean,
Without litter and graffiti on the walls.
I dream that this will make a better world.

I visualise that there should be more doctors
To help sick people.
I dream that this will make a better world.

I visualise that people will stop taking drugs
Because this will make people healthier.
I dream that this will make a better world.

I visualise that there should be no fast food restaurants
Like McDonald's. This will drop the level of obesity.
I dream that this will make a better world.

I visualise that families should not have arguments
That will cause the family to split up.
I dream that this will make a better world.

I visualise that schools should be less strict
About what religious people wear, eg, Muslims
Otherwise the religious person might get offended.
I dream that this will make a better world.

Anna Giles (14)
Newlands School, Seaford

Do Not Forget

Do not forget the hurt,
Do not forget the hunger,
I believe that the people in Africa dying, deserve to live,
I believe that we can stop this unbearable poverty.

Do not forget the world before wars,
Do not forget how the people flourished,
I believe that we can exist peacefully, in harmony,
I believe that we can live together in a faultless world.

Do not forget the elderly,
Do not forget the young,
I believe that we caused pain to both in wars,
I believe that we kindled this age of terror.

Do not forget that we can win,
Do not forget that we can prevail,
I believe that we can destroy the world of slavery,
I believe that we can free all the slaves to a life of independence.

Do not forget the happiness,
Do not forget the sadness,
I believe that there is a perfect world for everyone,
I believe that we can create a perfect world.

James O'Donnell (12)
Newlands School, Seaford

Think

Think, the world could be a better place
For the whole human race
If we could work together with a kindly face
And give each other time and space

Think, we use greed and war
To set ourselves above the law
All we want is more and more
So we are rich and others poor

Think, wouldn't it be great
If we stopped consuming at this appalling rate
And so saved the world from a dreadful fate?
It's not too late . . .

Think . . .

Timothy Waters (13)
Newlands School, Seaford

If Only

If only you could see what I do
You would be shocked about what happens around you
If only you could hear what I hear
You wouldn't run, you'd stay and fight what you fear

If only politicians could see what changes we can make
Then maybe we could give and not just take
If only in this world we could learn to trust
Our hopes and dreams not turned to dust

If only there wasn't such a thing as war
Then maybe we could all get up and open a new door
Things we love and hope to hold
Will move on fast and grow dusty and old.

Saskia Gunson (14)
Newlands School, Seaford

If I Had The World In The Palm Of My Hand

If I had the world in the palm of my hand
I would squeeze out the bad for evermore

If I had the world in the palm of my hand
I would look for the good and select the best

I would take what I found and spread it around
So that peace would be normal and war forced out

Life would be sweet and things would be shared
And no one would be without love and compassion

Greed and envy would be lost forever and all families united together
If I had the world in the palm of my hand.

Francesca Forde (13)
Newlands School, Seaford

My Dream

I have a dream where the poorest countries
are relieved of their debt,
and can use the money to build a richer life.

I have a dream where world hunger will be no more,
where we will have to see pictures of people
so thin it makes us cry.

I have a dream where people can provide for their families.
We become obese on burgers and chips,
while African people die of starvation and disease.

Next time you complain about your food,
be aware of how lucky you really are!

Philip Hersee (13)
Newlands School, Seaford

In My Eyes

Can't you hear the children's cries?
Can't you see the fear in their eyes?
Can't you see people asking for one more breath?
As they reach the minutes just before death
Families' homes burnt beyond repair,
While the smell of death hovers in the air.

Can you see the people living in fear
Because they know their death is near?
They only ask you to make peace,
They only want all wars to cease.
But all they get is lie after lie,
And they're all fed up of saying goodbye.

To the ones they've lost and loved so much,
Your strong ways are losing their touch.
No guns and drugs is all they seek,
Just look into the eyes of the weak
And you will see the fear in their eyes,
And you will hear and feel their cries.

These people live their life in fright,
Give them a way, show them the light.
Just help them believe, show them a sign,
Before you run out of valuable time,
Before the abuse and riots come,
Where young and old seize their guns.

So before the world starts a war,
Before people are found shot on the floor.
Think of how we can make it fair,
Show that we really do care.
Show people what they mean to you,
Earn their respect, think what you do!

Katy Feek (14)
Newlands School, Seaford

I Wish . . .

I wish that people were not judged
Say nasty things or hold a grudge.

I wish that pets weren't abandoned
If they do something wrong then they should be pardoned.

I wish that people would love and not hate
To care for things or talk to a mate.

I wish that the world was calm and peaceful,
Nothing is a rush, but very graceful.

I wish that poverty is totally wiped out,
People in hospitals would be cured, no doubt.

I wish that everyone's life is good and successful,
And children would play, help out and be useful.

I wish that my life will keep on going,
So I can see the world develop and keep on growing.

I wish that people would stop smoking,
It's not good for you, I'm not joking!

Nalissa Petfield (12)
Newlands School, Seaford

Just Imagine

Just imagine a better place,
Where it would not matter what colour or race.
Just imagine a world with enough food,
A world where people aren't arrogant and rude.

Just imagine a world without guns and drugs,
A place with no robbers and thugs.
Just imagine a place with lots of love,
I'm sure that that is wished from above.

Just imagine a place without fear,
A place where children don't drink beer.
Stop imagining and make it come true,
Maybe there are more people that think like you.

Nina Wiehrich (13)
Newlands School, Seaford

My Dream

My dream is a world where there is no hate
And pensioners can safely walk the streets when it's late.
Where everyone is loving, and not obsessed with war,
Where young people don't carry guns or knives anymore.
My dream is a world where everyone will share,
Everyone will love, and everyone will care.
Where everyone is equal and everything is just,
We'll all get along and find friends we can trust.
My dream is a world where poverty is no more,
Where homeless people have a house and don't sleep on the floor.
Where the streets aren't decorated with trash or gum,
Where people of other races aren't treated like scum.
My dream is close and within our reach,
Tell people about it, talk and teach.
Let's try it now for me and you.
Let's see if my dream really will come true.

Vicky Cowlett (12)
Newlands School, Seaford

My Picture

Picture going shopping and not having to lock your car.
Picture losing your bag and having it returned to you the next day
                                        with nothing missing.
Picture sitting in a café and there being no one smoking.
Picture walking along the street and not seeing a single piece
                                of chewing gum on the ground.
Picture all animals being treated nicely and not abandoned.

Picture everyone having a job that they really do like.
Picture every piece of litter to go in the bin and not on the floor.
Picture parents letting their kids go on the bus on their own.
Picture a newspaper being full of good things because there
                                is no bad news, only good.

Make my picture, the world's future.

Georgia Hunt (12)
Newlands School, Seaford

Live The Dream

I have a dream the poverty will be eliminated,
That people will be happy not devastated.

I have a dream that the homeless
Will have a roof over their heads,
Instead of the floor, a warm clean bed.

I have a dream that the children of Africa
Will have something good to eat,
That they have some shoes for their feet.

I have a dream that poor children will get good education
And that people will get along all around the nation.

I have a dream that pathways will be litter-free,
So that people won't trip and scrape their knees.

I have a dream that we all come together
And live this dream forever and ever.

Rachel Bonnici (12)
Newlands School, Seaford

I Have A Dream

I have a dream that sick children can live in safe homes.
I have a dream that a victim doesn't have to feel alone.
I have a dream that our streets can be clear of gum.
I have a dream that we can swim in a sea without dirt and scum.
I have a dream that we can live on just trust.
I have a dream that lies could turn to dust.
I have a dream that people judge you inside, not out.
I have a dream that more children would talk when they're in doubt.

If my dreams come true then the world will be perfect.
Stop living the nightmare.

Chloë Sanders (12)
Newlands School, Seaford

If Only . . .

If only the world could be a better place,
If only people knew they could be safe,
If only we could recognise the hurt ones,
If only we could feel secure at night.

If only pavements weren't layered with gum,
If only sunbathers could lie without rubbish,
If only we could recognise the mess we've made,
If only we could make the world a luxurious place.

If only we could stop the wars,
If only we could give more to others,
If only we could be more charitable to others,
If only we could stop the fights.

If only we could stop the terror,
If only we could stop the pollution,
If only we could stop the viciousness
And heal the pain and fear.

If only, if only . . .

Jasmine Munns (12)
Newlands School, Seaford

My Dream

Mountain boarding, I have a dream of being a professional.
I want to encourage others to get involved in a sport
That will help them overcome their fears of extreme sports.
Even though I have just started it but I think it is fun.
Other people are scared of heights.
When I first started to do it I was scared
That I would hurt myself and of the heights.
I did it in the end, I overcame my fear of getting on the hills.
So get involved with cool stuff.
You will like the stuff you try out.
Try sports like football and other physical stuff.
This is my dream.

Billy George (13)
Owlswick School, Lewes

I Had A Dream

I had a dream
It was happy as can be
Joy and openness
I love the no-war world

Terrorism out the window
Raping bored of
Shooting flies away
Speeding slows down

Ice caps grow again
And the Yellowstone Volcano falls asleep
Bullying finished
Fights gone

This is my dream and there is more,
Burglars are carried away,
Porn worn out
And happiness grows.

No locked doors,
No keys to rattle,
People open
Churches grow
Telling off turns to singing
Shouting turns to a whisper.

Matthew Kemp (14)
Owlswick School, Lewes

Tabloid Dreams

Forgive me if I dare to dream
Of British behaviour less obscene

I do not wish to cause offence
But I believe we've lost all sense

Other religions need not care
As the UK cries in silent despair

British tradition, for us, is denied
Whilst Blair is kissing other's behinds

Countries strict with culture, we must respect
A slight hypocrisy, I do detect

Why do we continue in ignorant bliss?
We are not holding prejudice

The government lacks democracy
We *all* have the right to British legacy

Political correctness has caused abrasions
'Police allow all but Caucasians'

So will you embrace the tabloids' dreams?
Don't pardon your children's nativity scenes

Go have your Christmas Day in style
Take your homo' partner up the aisle

Have your crosses at funerals
Let your kids sing hymns at school

Newspaper articles refuse to disguise
An old prime minister smothering lies

Will you follow the conspiracies blindly
Or unite to a universal society?

The gap between people and power joins
No Monarchy to take our copper coins

Lay down the laws of alienation
And stand side by side as one nation.

Rebecca Santos (18)
Park College, Eastbourne

I Have A Dream

Imagine
Enchanting music
Humming to you
Imagine
It's streaming through you
Imagine
Your heart racing
All your fear
All loose
Imagine
There's people joyfully laughing together
Imagine
You are smiling
Imagine
There's a sudden silence
'Slam'
Imagine
It's just got blurred, the camera you're holding drops
Imagine
You feel lost
Imagine
A faint voice says, 'Stop imagining you're dreaming,
Wake, wake waaakkeee up!'
Imagine
There's pictures going through your mind
Imagine
Distant memories
Where there's a warm glow
Imagine
You're completely relaxed
Imagine
There's nothing in your way
Imagine
You let your dreams take flight.

Rosemary Whitney (16)
Patcham House Special School, Brighton

I Have A Dream

I have a dream
To be a woman whose name everyone knows,
To move up and down, and be noticed,
To have the public admire my clothes and hair.

I want to win prizes, awards and Oscars,
To be the face in all of the newspapers,
To wave down the red carpet
In a glistening gown.

But I am only the school chef, all the students know,
I do win prizes: for the best cook,
And I do walk down the red carpets - to the kitchens,
But I want more.

I want to be the 'latest thing'
To have a smile that makes people go weak at the knees,
I want to be the most glamorous
But how can I in a dull blue dress?

I want to wake up being a 'somebody'
To sleep in a palace,
Knowing I am happy,
But alas, that never happens to me.

I will keep my dream
Forever and always
I sleep with my dream
But I wake up to reality.

Alice Phillips (14)
St Leonard's Mayfield School, Mayfield

I Have A Dream

I have a dream of being ambitious
Who cares what people think?
You only live once and that's the way God made us
So do what you want but just live!

I have a dream of being in the Amazon
Swinging from tree to tree
Colliding with exotic flowers and fruits
Beyond anyone's eyes or belief.

I have a dream of cascading down a waterfall
Turquoise, blues and greens
Feeling a thrust of life beneath your spirit
And landing in a pool of dreams.

I have a dream of climbing Mount Everest
The snow, ice and gleam.
The terror, fright, thrill of the unknown,
Witnessing what hasn't been seen.

I have a dream of riding camels in the desert
Among the golden grains of sand
Where the sun beams glorious rays of heat
In the isolated wondrous land.

I have a dream to fly away
To a world full of peace and love -
No war, pain, lies and deceit,
Just paradise in the sky above.

Liza Baucher (14)
St Leonard's Mayfield School, Mayfield

I Have A Dream

Usually my dreams are sound,
Calming and kind,
I feel I can drift away,
A new life within my mind.

My regular dreams are happy ones,
Relaxing like a soothing whale's song,
But sometimes, against my will,
My happy dreams go wrong.

They start like every other,
But take a turn for the worse,
Something terrible happens to me,
As if I am taken over by a curse.

My family are under attack,
I try to help them,
But there is no way
To free them from savage men.

I start to scream,
Feeling so very unkind.
I can't do anything,
I just wish I could turn off my mind.

In a cold sweat,
Grasping on,
But I'm falling, falling,
What have I done wrong?

I feel helpless,
I've brought everyone to harm,
But then a miracle happens,
The sound of my alarm!

Sophie Bowe (13)
St Leonard's Mayfield School, Mayfield

I Have A Dream

I have a dream,
To be a star.
My family thinks,
I could go far.

I haven't the money,
To buy the clothes.
I haven't the body,
To strut the pose.

I haven't the hair,
To look like magic.
Unfortunately my face,
Is rather tragic.

But I have the talent,
I could be great.
But there's no opportunity,
I'll have to wait.

Now the opportunity's,
Come around.
He takes one look
And then he frowns.

'Next!' he says,
And shoos me away.
My dream is over,
Thanks to today.

I have a dream,
What is to be?
But dreams never work
For people like me!

Charlotte Hutchinson (14)
St Leonard's Mayfield School, Mayfield

I Have A Dream

I have a dream of walking on a cloud of silver,
Fluffy candyfloss between my toes.
Suddenly I drop but feel my body lift up;
The wind whips through my hair.
I soar up through the sky and over the land below.

I glide over fields of gold
And happy children laughing,
I look down and see such
Harmony, happiness and love.

I fly further on around the world
And everywhere I go, all people are at peace,
The land untouched by human hands.

Although I feel calm, surreal and free,
I knew it can't last.
Soon I will have to return to the real world,

To misery, poverty, starvation and death,
I will have to see the truth that awaits me.
I will have to see a world not full of smiles
But full of hatred and war.

I have a dream of walking on a cloud of silver,
Where all is right with the world.

Alice Voke (13)
St Leonard's Mayfield School, Mayfield

I Have A Dream

I have a dream,
Of comfort and love,
One where delight and perfection
Rule the land from above.

I have a dream,
Of peace, not war.
Laughter and smiles,
Trouble and strife, no more.

I have a dream,
Where my joys run wild,
Only cries of love and laughter,
Or the giggle of a small child.

I have a dream,
With the sun's golden rays,
Grass, pure green,
With the sea and sky, blue, no grey.

I have a dream,
It's perfect but plain,
It's surreal yet alive,
Only as a dream it shall remain.

Eleanor McLaren (13)
St Leonard's Mayfield School, Mayfield

I Have A Dream

I have a dream
Of a world with honeysuckle and cherries,
With birds and bees, waterfalls and strawberries

I have a dream
Of a world with angelic summers and clean blue skies,
Of dewdropped fields and exotic dragonflies.

I have a dream
Of long, fulfilling lives, having someone to cherish
And love that never dies;
With passion, no regret and memories that will last,
A life that is complete and that doesn't fly past.

I have a dream
Of a mother holding her child's embrace,
Of brothers and sisters playing and seeing the smile
On their sibling's face.

I have a dream
Of a world where people are more thoughtful and wise,
Instead of our world, with jealousy, deceit and lies.

I have a dream
Of a world with love, happiness and security,
Not a world with hate, depression and difficulty.

I have a dream,
I have a dream,
That's all it is,
Just a dream.

Sefi Bagshawe (14)
St Leonard's Mayfield School, Mayfield

I Have A Dream

Imagined series of events,
This type of dream is always dreamt.
A cherished hope, a wonderful thing,
A dream is as long as a piece of string.

I have a dream which covers the world,
A vision, ambition, cannot be curled,
A dream of equality, of peace not war,
No people starving, what is it for?

A design, desire, a fantasy,
Where the rich give money to charity,
With the millionaires to share their cash,
We should be dumping hope and recycling trash.

Where it doesn't matter about your race,
Whether you're a girl, a boy or a disgrace.
We should all be treated the same,
There's no difference between the healthy and the lame.

Why are we cutting down trees for people to farm?
No war would spread if we were all calm.
The wildlife around you is a wonderful sign,
Of how pollution is changing our day and time.

In my dream, we all give love,
With hope spreading like a dove,
Where no one's killed, so no one dies,
A world where there's no need to cry.

Lucy Melia (12)
St Leonard's Mayfield School, Mayfield

I Have A Dream

As London lifts the Olympic flame,
High up in the sky,
Millions of eyes gaze up,
As the Olympic Games arrive.

Proudly representing my country,
Padded up in my goalkeeping kit,
My stomach fills with anticipation,
As I walk out onto the pitch.

The whistle has been blown,
The game has begun,
The ball has been hit,
Sticks have been swung.

An attacker approaches,
The defence has been got,
My pads deflect,
The ball that has been shot.

The coach gives us
A quick team talk,
Words of wisdom,
Give focus to our thoughts.

Time is called,
An injury has sprung,
A girl has been hit,
A substitute comes on.

The final whistle can be heard,
The stadium erupts.
The final game is over,
In joy my arms go up.

The British crowd,
Yell and scream,
Flying the Union flag,
This is my Olympic dream.

Alice Holden (13)
St Leonard's Mayfield School, Mayfield

I Have A Dream

I have a dream of a perfect world,
A world that isn't controlled by money
And people aren't riddled with the disease of deception,
But a world that's honest and true.

In this world everyone is happy,
It is safe for people to go out onto the streets,
Without the fear of being attacked
Or someone getting hurt.

I want a world with no guns and no bombs,
A world free of violence and murder,
Where no one is controlled
But everyone is a free spirit.

Everything in my world is flawless,
Except for one vital thing,
My world is only a dream
And won't ever come true.

Amber Gill (13)
St Leonard's Mayfield School, Mayfield

I Had A Dream

I had a dream that I was Miss America,
No one else, of me a replica.
I danced and I pranced,
I was queen of the stage.
My clothes and my make-up
Were all the rage.
Boys whistled in the street when passing by,
Hooting and tooting and heaving a sigh.
I was the envy of all my peers,
My lips, my nose, my eyes, my ears.
I was Miss America for a night,
That night everything was right!

Helen Bowen Wright (13)
St Leonard's Mayfield School, Mayfield

I Have A Dream

I have a dream,
That I will be in the Olympic team.

Swimming faster,
So that I will be the master.

Powering my arms,
As the water trickles down my palms.

Lifting them off the water,
So that I won't get slaughtered.

Now the tumble turn, the bit I can't do.
Gosh I really need a clue,

As to who is winning
Because my head is spinning.

I push off now the turn is over.
I sense a four-leaved clover,

As I push towards the end
And think about my friend,

Who is very sick,
So I give an extra kick.

I've won.
I've really, really won.

My friend will be so proud.

Katie Grainger (11)
St Leonard's Mayfield School, Mayfield

I Have A Dream

I have a dream,
That one day I will win a trophy
Of gleaming gold,
And bright red jewels
With my name inscribed
And with a cheque inside,
Of a million pounds,
To spend on anything,
From a brand new house,
To a washing line.

I'd win a race,
Against the face,
Of so much opposition,
Deafened by a cheering crowd,
The perspiration trickling from my brow.
Every breath, a conscious heave
And every step a relentless sprint.
As if by clockwork, I spring upon my feet.
So much frustration, disappointment
Goes before that fleeting fame.

Isobel Bushell (13)
St Leonard's Mayfield School, Mayfield

I Have A Dream

I have a dream,
A dream that my parents and my sister will live, will live for evermore.

I have a dream,
A dream that my cousins and relatives in India,
                           live a long and happy life.

I have a dream,
A dream that my grandparents, dead or alive live happily
And are pleased with what they have achieved in their life.

I have a dream,
A dream that I grow up and live my dream life.

I have a dream,
A dream that my friends do what they fantasise about.

I have a dream,
A dream that let's all of these dreams come true.

Alice Saldanha (11)
St Leonard's Mayfield School, Mayfield

I Have A Dream

I have a dream about happiness and world peace,
Racism, fighting and prejudice would all cease.

I wish for a world that's all nice and green,
Instead of polluting let's try and be clean!

I dream of recycling and more conservation,
To save the resources of each of our nations.

If only we had less work and more play,
More family time together each day.

I wish for more tolerance between one another,
From country to country, from sister to brother.

Love and respect fill our hearts with elation,
Make the world a better place for the next generation

Different nationalities, black or white people,
God made this world for us all to be equal.

Rosie Gaston (11)
St Leonard's Mayfield School, Mayfield

I Have A Dream

I have a dream that I could go back in time,
I could go back and correct what I have said if it was bad,
I have a dream that I could go back in time,
I could stop wars happening, and people dying for no reason,
I have a dream that I could go back in time,
I could stop car crashes from happening
So no innocent people would die,
I have a dream that I could go back in time
I could make everyone live in peace,
I have a dream I could go back in time
I could stop diseases setting in on people.
If someone got an illness I could make sure,
That they would get it checked out and removed before it's too late,
I have a dream I could go back in time
I could stop arguments from happening,
I have a dream I could go back in time
I could stop people committing suicide,
I have a dream I could go back in time
I could stop people taking drugs then getting addicted,
I have a dream that I could go back in time
That is my dream!

Emma Graham (13)
St Leonard's Mayfield School, Mayfield

I Have A Dream

I have a dream that everyone can be,
A great, big, happy family.
With no more fighting and no more wars,
Where people abide by the laws.

Where people are in no particular place,
Or are different just because of their race.
It doesn't matter whether you're black or white.
We are all the same except what we look like.

No more threats and no more killing.
The world would be better if people were willing.
No more stealing, lots of faith,
Then the world will be safe.

I have a dream that everyone can be
A great big happy family.
With no more fighting and no more wars,
Where people abide by the laws.

Lily Cottle (11)
St Leonard's Mayfield School, Mayfield

They Had The Dream

He had the dream to change the world
And stop racism now
But all because of what he believed
All he got was death.

She had the dream to change the world
And people would follow her steps
To help and care for all those who were sick
And aid the ones who were injured.

They had the dream to change the world
To stop racism and help
To be remembered for what they have done
And forever loved for their care

Do you have the dream to change the world?
To stop and racism and help?
Would you put in action what you believe
And help all those who need it?

Emily Wright (13)
Sandford Middle School, Wareham

Terrorists

Without any terrorists there'll be no bombs,
I don't know why they're here.
Every day terrorists destroy homes and kill people,
They scare people from coming out of their homes.

Without any bombs there'll be no destruction,
I don't know why they're here.
Every day bombs take people's lives away and destroy homes,
They scare people from coming out of their homes.

Jake Muscato (11)
Sandford Middle School, Wareham

Imagine

People getting called names,
People getting killed,
People getting bullied at school,
Just because of their skin colour.

Imagine the world without all this,
People being nice,
People still alive,
Just because of their background.

People's homes getting destroyed,
All their valuables gone,
People getting killed,
Just because of their religion.

Imagine the world without all this,
No homes getting destroyed,
No people getting killed,
Just because of their beliefs.

Courtney Best (12)
Sandford Middle School, Wareham

I Have A Dream

Poverty shall be over,
No one will die every 3 seconds,
There will be no lack of food, clothes or water.

There shall be no racism,
Different skin colours shall be equal,
There will be no violent attacks.

I have a dream where everything is beautiful,
No war, no pollution and no poverty,
Rival countries shall not fight.

There shall be peace on Earth!

Mike Rice (12)
Sandford Middle School, Wareham

I Have A Dream

People suffer, they shouldn't,
People starve, they shouldn't,
People are killed, they shouldn't,

They should be free of pain and suffering,
They should be free of starvation and prejudice,
We are all equal whether we are black, white,
Chinese, Arabic, Jewish, French,
Kenyan, Indian, fat, thin
For we bear no difference to each other
And we are all the same people,

People murder, we can stop this?
People are homeless, we can stop this?
People commit crime, we can stop this?

The problem is that people are killers
And in this life,
We can stop this,
All it takes,
Is a small little dream,
A little dream to change it all.

Henry Watkins (12)
Sandford Middle School, Wareham

Sweets

I had a dream
Of a world of sweets,
Made of cream
Were the roads and streets.

In every house
And every flat
There was no mouse
That wasn't fat!

Chocolate for lunch
Candy for tea
Everyone had a crunch
Even a flea.

They had to stop crunching
Sweets were too bad!
They had to stop munching
For all that they had.

And then the dream stopped
I thought of our men
And my poor head popped
I had to save them!

Monica Bollani (13)
Sandford Middle School, Wareham

I Have A Dream

I have a dream that one day this world will be fair,
Everyone will care if something goes wrong
And not just those that are affected.
Poverty, unfairness and racism will not appear in anyone's dictionary,
Rich and poor will merge together, no one richer than the other.
Silly money won't be spent on football stars
When half the world is starving.
As one boy once said, 'I'm starving, you hold talks,
I'm still starving, you hold conferences and at the end it's too late'.
Promises are made by many world leaders,
But little, if any are kept.
Why doesn't Blair solve his own problems instead of 'helping' in Iraq,
Many of Britain's problems get pushed aside labelled 'not important'.
People get accused, sometimes killed
Because they have a certain belief,
Everyone has beliefs, so why are only certain ones killed?
Terrorism is now common, taking many innocent ones with it.
Murders happen frequently just because individuals look different,
It just goes to show how shambolic the world is,
But in my world, hatred and wrongdoing are only a myth,
Because in my world peacefulness and happiness
Fill the world and hearts of everyone,
Forgiveness won't be needed as nobody will commit wrongdoings,
That's my dream,
But until a miracle comes - that remains only a dream.

Tom Rolls (12)
Sandford Middle School, Wareham

Poverty

I have a dream that happened last night,
It wasn't very nice and it gave me a fright,
All the little children that were ill in every bed,
'Help! Help! Help!' That was all that was said.

I have a dream they all got more food,
Someone to help to put them out of their mood,
Things to do, something to see,
All they need is a key to be free.

I have a dream they all got more treatment,
To them it will be like getting a present,
Their sad little faces will turn to a smile,
At least they'll get help once in a while.

I have a dream that poverty will end,
That together the countries will blend,
The greed will stop,
So give poverty the chop!

Lauren Adams (13)
Sandford Middle School, Wareham

I Have A Dream

I have a dream, there shall be peace on Earth.
I have a dream, there shall be no bullying.
I have a dream, there shall be a truce between us and Iraq.
I have a dream, there shall be no more cruelty to humans and animals.
I have a dream, there shall be no poverty.
I have a dream, the world will be a cleaner environment.
I have a dream, there shall be no painful death.
I have a dream, there shall be freedom
Of speech, expression and emotion.
I have a dream,
I have a dream.

Ryan King (12)
Sandford Middle School, Wareham

Make Poverty History

Make poverty history,
Everyone can help.
Feed the hungry,
Help the homeless.

The earthquakes, the hurricanes,
Losing their lovers
And then their children,
Make a difference in the world.

Why does God let this happen?
Why does he put people in misery?
Taking people's homes,
Supplying them with doubt.

Let the people live a fair life,
Living in the streets,
With rubble zooming everywhere,
Sad and crying faces, all over the world.

Do something great,
Give them a home,
Instead of the disasters,
Make poverty history!

Stephen Pope (12)
Sandford Middle School, Wareham

I Have A Dream

I have a dream of peace among men.
I have a dream of peace, joy and friends among others.
I have a dream of no wars, no death and no suffering.
I have a dream of friends among everyone.
I have a dream of happiness and kindness to others,
No arguing, death or suffering.
I have a dream of lost souls returning kindness to others.
I have a dream of safety, security.
I have a dream and it is a beautiful dream,
Now share it with me.

William Foster (12)
Sandford Middle School, Wareham

I Have A Dream

I have a dream
To stop world poverty
I have a dream
To stop world wars
I have a dream
To arrest all the guilty
I have a dream
To help the poor
I have a dream
To help the soldiers
I have a dream
To help the discriminated
I have a dream
To help victims
I have a dream
To save the world.

Ben Honeywill (12)
Sandford Middle School, Wareham

I Had A Dream

I had a dream . . .
where people all lived in peace.
I had a dream . . .
where poverty did not exist.
I had a dream . . .
where there was no jealousy and envy.
I had a dream . . .
but dreams are meant to be broken.

Oliver Walters (12)
Sandford Middle School, Wareham

I Have A Dream

I have a dream,
Racism is no more,
There is no difference
Between rich and poor.

I have a dream,
The world comes as one,
Poverty is over,
Over and done!

I have a dream,
I'll have one every night,
I open my eyes
And see this dreadful sight.

People don't smile,
People will get hurt,
Animals not free to roam
And roll in the dirt!

The world will be evil,
Terrorists walk free,
If only we'd look
And first see!

Racism still happening,
Poor treated less,
Poverty still existing,
When will the world confess?

I had a dream
I'll have a million more,
At least I opened my eyes
And this is what I saw.

Layla Norris (13)
Sandford Middle School, Wareham

We All Have The Dream

We all have the dream,
To change what's wrong,
To make the wrongs right.

We all have the dream,
To stop racism and war,
To create equality and peace.

We all have the dream,
To help those that cried,
The tears for the family.

We all have the dream,
To find those lost,
To help them find their way.

We all have the dream,
To speak out against hate,
Deceit, death, lies.

We all have the dream,
To be heard,
To be known.

We all have the dream,
To create dreams,
To end those nightmares,
That most people have to live every day.

We all have the dream,
Every one of us,
It's time to make it reality.

Becky Maidment (13)
Sandford Middle School, Wareham

I Had A Dream

I had a dream that there were no endangered species.
That there were no guns to kill and no knives
All animals had peace between each other.
Humans didn't have hatred kept inside.
No evil at all.

I had a dream that there was no poverty and no sadness.
Tears had been forgotten and revenge had not been caused
Alcohol was a long way away and there were no drugs.
Hatred was a feeling long forgotten and Hell was gone.
Happiness was the feeling of the millennium.

I had a dream that there was no swearing
And mankind knew only love
I felt a warm feeling of passionate joy
Guilt was gone with no one stealing.

I had a dream that there was no need for policemen
The weak were helped by the strong.
No diseases were about to destroy lives of the innocent
Prisons were a myth and no country was at war.

I had a dream about all that I've written
But it was a dream, it will never happen
Fright and fear is what the young and defenceless
Have had to put up with.
No one is safe in this world.

Jack Harcourt (11)
Sandford Middle School, Wareham

I Have A Dream

I have a dream for racism to stop
A total ban to all and the friendship to start
I have a dream that poverty will end
For crops to grow and famine to be exterminated
I have a dream for bullying to be confronted
For the dreams of little ones to be revived
I have a dream for all countries to be at peace
For them to help one another and religion is not a reason to have wars
I have a dream for pollution to stop
The o-zone to be revived and out of harm's way
I have a dream for animals to be free, not be tested on!
I have a dream for gang wars to end
The guns lowered and the happiness raised
I have a dream for sickness to stop
All cancers cured, viruses conquered
I have a dream for all forms of abuse to be long, forgotten history
For children frightened of their parents to be once again happy
I have a dream for the blind to see the wonderful countryside
The deaf to hear the tiny birds sing and the crippled to walk
I have a dream for victims of road killers to wake back up
To look after their families
I have a dream for money not to be important
To stomp down crime, a solution to murder
I know these won't come true but if you don't have a dream
How do you expect a dream to come true?

Anton Appleton (12)
Sandford Middle School, Wareham

I Have A Dream

I have a dream that racism should stop,
Because people are treating others unfairly
And it's getting on my nerves.
So the world is coming to an end for some,
But it won't if we stop it now.

Let's think about others for once
To see how lucky we are,
Here are some threatening words,
Kill, death, rape, racist and *blood,*
But we can move these words out of the way,
And produce better ones like
Happy, hello, equal, friendly.

When I see this behaviour,
It makes me feel sick, sad, lucky and disgraced,
By the way they treat others
And let's catch those racist people
And turn them inside out
To see the other side of that human.

Thomas Houlding (12)
Sandford Middle School, Wareham

I Have A Dream

I have a dream that everything will be okay,
Things will be good not bad,
I have a dream that racism will be stopped,
I wonder what would happen if it did?

I have a dream that the world will be peaceful,
No violence, no shouting . . . nothing,
I have a dream that no children will be on the streets,
I want them to all have a home.

I have a dream, I have a dream,
Tell me, tell me, what's your dream?

Melanie Welsh (12)
Sandford Middle School, Wareham

I Have A Dream

I have a dream,
I see no more wars of any sort.

I have a dream,
I see no more bombs harming others.

I have a dream,
I see animals no longer being badly treated.

I have a dream,
I see families spending time with each other.

I have a dream,
I see no more poverty in the world.

I have a dream,
I see hope, faith and love.

That's my dream!

Rosie Coombs (12)
Sandford Middle School, Wareham

I Have A Dream

I have a dream,
Where the world doesn't scream,
For us to stop destroying its beauty.

I have a thought,
Where the world isn't wrought,
With the everlasting scars of our greed.

I have a dream,
Where the world doesn't seem
To be punishing us for what we've done.

I have a thought,
Where the world isn't sought,
For the nature to satisfy our gluttony.

I hope my dreams come true.

Jack Cullimore (12)
Sandford Middle School, Wareham

I Have A Dream

I have a dream
That there will be no wars,
That everyone will live in peace
Getting along like one happy family.

I have a dream
That there will be no racism,
Black and white will all be the same.

I have a dream
That there will be no poverty,
Everybody will be able to afford what they need.

I have a dream
That there will be no natural disasters,
So no country will suffer.

I have a dream
That there will be no need for police,
Everywhere you go will be safe.

I have a dream,
I have a dream,
I have a dream.

Danielle Hewitt (12)
Sandford Middle School, Wareham

I Have A Dream

I lay awake cold and alone,
The Earth is an island, which I can't call home,
Everyone round me is dying,
I just can't help it, I just keep crying.

Why do we make fun of the colour of their face?
Why do we make fun of them and shout at their race?
It doesn't matter whether we are rich or have fame
Because after all we are all the same.

Nicola Parry (11)
Sandford Middle School, Wareham

Imagine A World . . .

Imagine a world where everyone's the same,
Skin, hair and eye colour,
Imagine a world without discrimination,
Today racism will be brought to an end.

Imagine a world where everyone's the same,
Skin, hair and eye colour,
Imagine a world where everyone was friends,
No war, no fight or terrorist attacks.

Imagine a world where everyone's the same,
Skin, hair and eye colour,
Imagine a world where everyone lived,
No killing, no bullying or dying.

Imagine a world where everyone's the same,
Skin, hair and eye colour,
Imagine a world where everyone has food,
No starving, no hunger or thirst.

Kerry Jarvis (12)
Sandford Middle School, Wareham

I Have A Dream

I have a dream that there will be forgiving and forgetting,
There will be no cruelty to animals
And no murders or terrorists.

Another dream I have is that there will be no wars,
No racism and no bombs.

My last dream I have
Is that there will be kindness all around the world,
Happiness, *yes!*
Sadness, *no!*

Carly-Jade Mason (11)
Sandford Middle School, Wareham

Suffering

Sometimes I think if I were in charge,
I would take away the cries of pain and fear,
Then I would stop the war
And make peace bigger than before.

Maybe it might stop, I don't know
It might be a long wait,
'Til people know what it's like,
But it's too late to hate.

It might have taken half the world,
How long will it carry on for?
But once it's gone we won't want more,
So let's go now and help those people.

Poverty might be gone,
Although sometimes it's a con,
Why do people lie,
When people are out there about to die?

Wars have been around,
For as long as I know
Innocent people are out there dying,
I wish it would decease and go.

Why do people have to beg,
For just one grain of rice?
Even though they earn money,
People just want more.

Without all these things,
Life would be better,
We wouldn't hear all those cries
And less people would die.

Anna Rowe (12)
Sandford Middle School, Wareham

I Have A Dream . . .

I have a dream . . .
One day it won't matter if you're black or white,
There will be peace on Earth
Shelter to all.

I have a dream . . .
There will be no bombing countries,
No war in Iraq
And no natural disasters.

I have a dream . . .
There will be no bullying,
No killing
And no pollution.

I have a dream . . .
There will be no endangered animals,
No damaging the environment
And no discrimination to all.

I have a dream . . .
Animals will no longer be killed for fur,
There will be no violence
And no deadly diseases.

I have a dream . . .
All the bad things in the world,
Turn to good things.
I have a dream.

Lauren Holder (13)
Sandford Middle School, Wareham

I Wish . . .

I wish the world could be at one with each other,
No war . . . just peace and harmony.
I wish the fighting and killing would stop,
Instead of going completely barmy.
I wish that people would think of what they are doing
And try to change the rules,
I wish one day people would think about their lives
And stop acting like complete and utter fools.

I wish people would remember the times,
When people lost their loved ones,
I wish people would remember the times,
When children screamed out for their mums.
I wish people would remember the times,
When bloody stench hung in the air,
I wish people would remember the times,
When at last you knew no one was there.

I wish people would stop being so arrogant
And at last face the facts,
I wish people would understand,
That there was no going back.
I wish people would learn from their mistakes
And try to change the future,
I wish people knew how so brave,
Those courageous soldiers were.

At the end of the day, all that has happened . . .
Is pain, torture and death.

Rebecca Howman (13)
Sandford Middle School, Wareham

I Had A Dream . . .

I had a dream that the world was clean of drugs,
That no longer innocent people's lives were taken over by addiction.

I had a dream that the world was clean of discrimination,
Black and white could live together as a community
As race was no longer an issue.

I had a dream that the world was clean of bullying,
Children would no longer be scared to walk outside their front door,
Or walk into school,
Children could live their lives free of fear.

If only my dream was real,
Everyone could live in peace,
The world could be free of worry and confusion.
I can only dream that this will come true.

Elisha Tagart (13)
Sandford Middle School, Wareham

I Have A Dream

I have a dream where violence is an illusion
And war has been chucked in the bin.

I have a dream where poverty is not a word
And hunger is a thing of the past.

I have a dream where there's no space for crime
And children don't suffer from abuse.

I have a dream where world peace has been made
And generosity is second nature.

I have a dream where happiness is never-ending
And sadness is not thought of.

I have a dream and now to ensure it becomes a reality.

Matt Sadler (12)
Sandford Middle School, Wareham

I Have A Dream

I had a dream that the world would become peaceful while
I was young, but it was shattered by drugs and terrorists,
So now I can only hope, that the next generation enjoy
Their childhood. So make it like that, how hard can it be?

I have a dream that the world will be peaceful,
I have a dream that the hatred will rest,
I have a dream that everyone will have a good life,
Not die when only 12 and that be their best.

I have a dream that poverty will vanish,
Then money won't mean a thing,
No rich or poor, no hate just love
Respecting all gods, wanting no king.

I don't want any discrimination,
I want all prejudice to go,
There isn't any difference, between black or white,
Why can't the love just flow?

If everyone could spare a handful of kindness,
There wouldn't be any ill,
No hunger, thirst or homeless,
Then no one would feel the chill.

Imagine what a difference it would make,
If the world was pure and clean,
People could relax and enjoy it,
And that's my only dream!

Ben Davies (12)
Sandford Middle School, Wareham

My Dream

I have a dream for the world
I hope it will become a lovely place
And everybody will enjoy living in their environment.

I have a dream for people on the streets
I hope they will recover and find
Exactly what they need.

I have a dream for animals
That they will be kept safe
And never get harmed.

I have a dream for pets
That they will be treated
As we would like to be treated.

I have a dream for friendship
That it stays among us forever
And never ceases.

I have a dream for the scared
That they will not be frightened
They will have more confidence
And reach out for what they want.

I have a dream for the lonely
I hope they will think about those
They need and talk to them about it.

If I had one wish
It would be to protect the poor, rich and lonely forever
And to make them happy.

Katie England (12)
Sandford Middle School, Wareham

I Have A Dream

I have a dream that everyone will be fair,
The birds will sing and people chatter,
I have a dream that the world is peaceful,
Where people grow old with happiness and love,
I have a dream that people will give,
That no one is selfish and unwelcome,
I have a dream that everyone's respected,
Where people pick up that bit of litter,
I have a dream that no one wants to kill,
And nobody can live in fear and disgrace,
I have a dream that there is no longer racism,
So you can walk down the street and it doesn't matter,
I have a dream that there is no poverty,
That everyone has enough money to live,
I have a dream that no child is ever beaten,
So that they live without worry,
I have a dream that everyone gives help,
Even if it doesn't look like they need any,
I have a dream that no one is a bully,
And they live with pride and joy,
I have a dream, I have a dream,
Because that's what life is about.

Amelia Elms (12)
Sandford Middle School, Wareham

I Have A Dream

I have a dream that everyone will be equal
That hunger in the world will fade
That people can be people instead of dying creatures
And that the world will be fair again.

I have a dream that water will flow in Africa
So that people can swim in the streams
So the rain will fall on children's hands
And make them feel that the world's at peace.

I have a dream that children won't be cold at night
That they will have blankets and heating to keep them warm
That they will have clothes for night and day
To cover their worn out skin
And to stop their little hands being cold

I have a dream that poverty will be over
That war and fighting will be put to rest
And that everyone will be equal
And live in a world that cares

I have a dream . . .
I hope one day everyone will see . . .

Chloe Spore (12)
Sandford Middle School, Wareham

I Have A Dream

I have a dream,
That all wars will end
And poverty will be washed away.

I have a dream,
That cruelty to children will stop
And the rich will give to the homeless and poor.

I have a dream,
That there will be no starvation in the world,
That everyone has a home in which to live.

I have a dream,
That there will be no pollution,
That the world will become more environmentally friendly.

I have a dream,
That all hunting is banned
And that there is no cruelty to animals.

I have a dream,
That bad will become good,
I have a dream,
I have a dream.

Lucy Barfoot (11)
Sandford Middle School, Wareham

I Have A Dream

I have a dream,
That repeats every night,
I dream I wake up but each night is a different night.

I have a dream,
A dream where time stops
And I'm taken round the world.

I have a dream,
I travel through the carnage,
See death and chaos.

I have a dream,
There I see people suffer
And where poverty takes its toll.

I have a dream,
Where I see disease
And families dying.

I have a dream,
These things are just in my dream
And not in the world that surrounds me.

Alex Boyd (12)
Sandford Middle School, Wareham

I Have A Dream

I have a dream that when I'm older,
There will be no more poverty,
Everyone will have enough food to eat
And enough water to drink.

There will be no discrimination or prejudice,
Black and white people will be equal
And there will be no such word as racism.

There will be no terrorists,
No bombs, no wars, no explosions - just peace,
The army won't be needed, as there won't be any wars.

Knives will only be used for cooking,
No one will ever be stabbed or hurt again
And guns will never be fired, aimed or shot at anyone again.

That rainforests won't be cut down,
Animals' habitats will still be there in 10 years time
And poaching/hunting will stop.

That the world won't be polluted,
The environment will be clean
And global warming will stop.

Emily Witham (11)
Sandford Middle School, Wareham

What A World

What a world we live in
When a man can kill another
What a world we live in
When a country can invade a country
What a world we live in
When the money is kept from the poor
What a world we live in
When people live on the streets
What a world we live in
When black and white are at war
What a world we live in
When people are abusing their bodies with drugs
What a world we live in
When people drown their souls with alcohol
What a world we live in
When people abuse the environment
What a world we live in
When pain and hunger can go unnoticed
What a world we live in
When people are killed for their beliefs
What a world we live in
When a dream of a world where everything can live in peace
Is nothing more than a dream.

Steven Churchill (12)
Sandford Middle School, Wareham

I Have A Dream

I have a dream that the world will be peaceful,
No war, no fighting or bullying,
I have a dream that everyone will be kind and sharing,
No money, no poverty or no greed,

I have a dream that everyone will be happy,
No disappointment or unhappiness,
I have a dream that there will be no prejudice or discrimination,
No black, no white, or unfairness,

I have a dream that there will be no cruelty,
To children, the elderly or animals,
I have a dream that people can be safe,
In their homes, on the streets or on public transport,

I have a dream that there will be no illnesses,
No diseases, no germs or injuries,
I have a dream that there will be no disabled people,
No blind, no deaf or dumb.

Michael Goff (11)
Sandford Middle School, Wareham

I Wish

I wish everyone would stop fighting, there is no reason for it,
Innocent people dying because of disagreements.
I wish poverty would end, we could do better without it,
People living on the streets, begging for bits of food.
I wish bullying would decease, there is no point having it,
People getting picked on for the way they look.
I wish racism would finish, we could live without it,
Everyone is exactly the same inside, they just have different beliefs.

If all of the problems in the world would end,
Everyone would be happy and cheerful
And the world would be a better place to live in.

Kayleigh Noyce (13)
Sandford Middle School, Wareham

I Have A Dream

I have a dream,
Of no world wars,
There will be everlasting peace,
Through all mankind.

I have a dream,
Every man will be respected,
And not be picked on,
For their looks or beliefs.

I have a dream,
No animals are endangered,
There is no racism
And no nuclear missile attacks.

I have a dream,
I hope it comes true,
The world would be better,
I have a dream.

Robert Spivey (11)
Sandford Middle School, Wareham

I Have A Dream . . .

I have a dream,
I wish for love,
I wish for hope, spirit and a companion.

I have a dream,
I wish for no litter,
I wish for no pollution, animal danger and poverty.

I have a dream,
I wish that people would make the world a better place
And that those people would stop splitting up their families,
Stop mistreating animals and help the poor people survive!

I have a dream but life is no better.

Esmé Phillips (12)
Sandford Middle School, Wareham

I Have A Dream

I have a dream that everyone can believe in themselves,
That people will respect people for who they are, not what they are.
I have a dream that everyone will be treated equally,
Black and white should become one to make the world a better place.
I have a dream that money will not take over the world,
Greed and gluttony will be extinct.
I have a dream that everyone should have the same rights,
From rights to eat, to the right to an education.
I have a dream that justice will be done to everybody
And everything on this Earth,
People will learn to live, assist and respect one another.
I have a dream that all races, religions and communities
Will all become fond of their fellow human beings.
I have a dream without poverty and famine
A person's health will be as equally good as the next.
I have a dream that people will not abuse their bodies,
Alcohol and drugs only bring pain and hurt.
I have a dream that everyone will be who they want to be
When they are older,
This ambition should not be driven by the force of greed.
I have a dream that everyone will live their life to the full,
We shouldn't be monotonous, we only have one life.
I have a dream that people should question
What is being done to the world,
If in doubt do something about it.
I have a dream that the sun will rise to a better world,
I have a dream that my dreams will become your dreams too.

Ben Newton (13)
Sandford Middle School, Wareham

I Have A Dream

I have a dream,
That there will be no war, evil or pain,
The way forward, there is a lot to gain.

I have a dream,
That there will be good, happiness and love,
To people on Earth and Heaven above.

I have a dream,
That there will be no sickness, litter or madness,
There will be world peace and no sadness.

I have a dream,
That there will be happiness all around,
In the sky and on the ground.

Jenna Dick (12)
Sandford Middle School, Wareham

I Have A Dream

I have a dream to kick racism out the window
To aid the unfortunate with three banquets a day
To flush poverty down the dirty drains
To push bullying away from the crowd
And to let kindness and loyalty join in.

I have a dream to get rid of name-calling
To keep child abuse out of our lives
To wash away the people that put you down
To pull the plug on sexism
And to let consideration show us the way.

And I know if all this would happen
The world would be living a dream.

Nat Scott (13)
Sandford Middle School, Wareham

I Have A Dream . . .

One day it will happen,
The lies will subside
And the truth will come out.

Why do ordinary people have to suffer because of others?
What did they do?
What did they say?

Why are people greedy, why do they steal?
What do they want?
What can you do?

How can we help the less fortunate people?
What needs to be done?
What needs to be said?

Why is there racism?
Why is there war?
What can be done, to put an end to it all?

One day it will happen,
I promise you this,
The lies *will* subside
And the truth *will* come out!

Ryan Pannell (12)
Sandford Middle School, Wareham

We Can Make It Right

We can make it right,
The lives of others are in our hands.
We can let them live
And help them to continue.
Let them live in peace.
We can make it right,
To stop pointless confrontation
With a single word,
A simple apology
Can stop the meaningless death.
We can make it right,
To keep our world pure,
To make it beautiful,
For our children of tomorrow.
Don't let them live in darkness.
We can make it right,
To stop the hate
And discrimination of others,
We look different for a reason,
We look different for individuality.

Sophie Terrell (13)
Sandford Middle School, Wareham

I Have A Dream

I stand there,
With a broken heart,
All I can hear is the noise of the trees whistling,
I wish my dream could come true,
That the world would become a better place,
With no drugs, violence or rudeness,
And everyone would get along,
So people would not get picked on,
If they were different religions or skin colour,
Or people would not die of hunger.

I wish my dream could come true,
That the world would become a better place,
Like many people in the earthquake lost their families,
And have no shelter or home,
And might not survive from sleeping on streets,
Like many people from newborn to old,
Have died from an earthquake,
Just like the natural tsunami,
Which destroyed lots of houses
And thousands of people die of a natural disaster.

I wish my dream could come true,
That the world will become a better place,
By being friendly and kind,
Whatever religion or skin colour
And let people be free,
So they are allowed to make friends
And try and stop the natural disasters,
By trying to make the world a better place,
So people will not be so violent, rude and take drugs,
So all these disasters will not happen
And so my dream will come true,
That the world will become a better place.

Catherine Atwell (12)
Sandford Middle School, Wareham

I Have A Dream

I have a dream of the world without people breaking the law.
I have a dream of a world free from poverty.
I have a dream of the world in complete peace.
I have a dream of a world free of people
Killing other people for no reason.
I have a dream of the world without people taking drugs
And people binge drinking.
I would have a world without people dying of old age or illness.
I have a dream of a world without people being hurt
Whenever they go to turn around the street corner!
I have a dream of the world without being short changed
When you get your shopping from the local shop.
I have a dream of a world without children
Carrying guns and knives around.
I have a dream of a world without going home
And finding out you have been burgled.

Stacey Watkins (12)
Sandford Middle School, Wareham

I Have A Dream

If you have a dream
You should stick with it
Cos if you don't keep this world, who will?

Who will destroy all evil?
Who will stop wars and destruction?
Who will make this world a better place for everyone,
Whether they be black or white?
So never give up, because if you do everyone will.

You represent everyone
And everyone represents the world.
We only get one chance on this Earth, use it well.

Never give up because the moment you give up,
Will be the moment the world gives up.
You can't make a difference if you're not here.

Liam Sykes (13)
Sandford Middle School, Wareham

I Have A Dream . . .

I dream that one day the world will fall silent
The cries of pain will be a distant memory
The pleas for help will be answered
And all will be calm.

I dream that one day we will all live in peace
The cancer of racism that gnaws away at us will be overcome
All will be equal and treated with respect
United under one god.

I dream that one day the downtrodden will be uplifted
The grieving will find peace
The lost will find leadership
And the despairing will be led to the sunshine of eternal hope.

Humans by nature fight to the end
We keep getting bigger weapons, bigger wars, bigger problems
It takes thousands of people to create a society
But just a few to send it crashing to the ground.

In the end everyone loses.

I hope my prayers will be answered
I hope that my dreams will come true
But I am now slowly realising
That my dream is just that - a dream.

Bethany Willmot (13)
Sandford Middle School, Wareham

I Have A Dream . . .

I have a dream that countries won't fight,
I have a dream that fires won't ignite.
I have a dream that when you pass people in need,
I have a dream you'll let go of your greed.

I have a dream poverty will end,
I have a dream that millions will be sent.
I have a dream children won't be crying,
I have a dream people aren't dying.

I have a dream that this will all stop,
I have a dream that it's always a good crop,
I have a dream good words are spoken,
I have a dream no bones are broken.

I have a dream we won't have to lie,
I have a dream we won't have to say goodbye.
I have a dream people are free,
I have a dream those people can live like you and me.

I have a dream animals won't perish,
I have a dream there will still be fish.
I have a dream that forests won't catch fire,
I have a dream I can still hear the choir.

I have a dream, a little insignificant dream,
I have a dream that this poem isn't what it seems.

Daisy Brock (13)
Sandford Middle School, Wareham

I Have A Dream

Upon this world there's more than one race,
It doesn't matter about the colour on their face,
Why do they get shouted at, usually get called names,
Why can they not see, inside we're all the same?
We all live together in this world,
Though people on streets lay there cold.
People killing, people dying,
Families mourning whilst they're crying.
Think about people who live on the street,
Not knowing how to make two ends meet!
It really doesn't matter if you're black or white,
Just think of a world where no one would fight.
If you just think about this for a while,
You may even make a young orphan smile.
I hate to see those people in pain,
But who can they turn to, who can they blame?
Some celebs are full of greed,
But some, to the orphans they give money to feed.
If we just help parents not to fight,
You will give a child a smile tonight.
If this poem has touched you deep inside,
The main two nations won't need to collide!

Lauren Peters (12)
Sandford Middle School, Wareham

I Wish . . .

I wish I could change the world
The world that is sickened with poverty
The lack of food
The dirty water
The homeless families
With no clothes on their back.

I wish I could change the world
The world that is full with racism
The boy who got killed with an axe
To getting abused on a bus
I hope this doesn't happen again
I wish the world could be friends again.

I wish I could change the world
The world that is full with conflict
The war in Iraq to the bombings in London
People getting hurt, people getting killed.

I wish I could change the world
So we are one big family
No poverty, no racism, no conflict
Just one big happy family.

Emily Gale (12)
Sandford Middle School, Wareham

I Had A Dream

It doesn't really matter whether you're black or white.
Don't run away, we don't bite
Just because I am a different colour just believe in me.
I wish we were one big family

I wish we were one big family
Can you imagine a world without poverty?
I wish I had all the money in the world,
So I could make people less cold.
If only people had some spare money
To build houses for the poor
Then people wouldn't sleep on the cold floor.

Can you imagine not being able to read?
So then you will not be able to feed.
Can you imagine having dirty water
Or a life full of slaughter?

Can you imagine not having a mum or dad?
Every day you would be so sad
Can you imagine being a slave
Or at 12 being in a grave?

Can you imagine making someone smile?
You can make someone not sleep on a cold tile
It doesn't really matter whether you are black or white,
Don't run away, we don't bite.

Gareth Eyles (12)
Sandford Middle School, Wareham

I Have A Dream . . .

I have a dream, a big, big dream
That the world would be in perfect harmony.
No anger, no war.
But freedom is won by anyone, any animal is free.
But no one is free, nothing is free.
Nothing!

But if everything was free, this world would not be a world.
A world is built up of imperfect things.

You earn everything, food, money, land
That makes life worth living.

But if everything was perfect there would be wars all over
No one would share anything.

We own things to improve our lives
But some people don't have anything, so how can they share?

If we had harmony I agree it would be a better place
But this world is the best we can get
So let's share it whilst we can.

I dream that this world would be perfect
But how can it be perfect when there is no such thing?

But this world would never be good enough for us.
Is there any such thing as a perfect world?

Emma Vinson (13)
Sandford Middle School, Wareham

I Have A Dream

I have a dream, a little, tiny dream
We're last in the Premiership
We're another man down.

I have a dream, a little, tiny dream
We're last to be thought about
We're never meant to speak.

I have a dream, a little, tiny dream
We're starving, hungry
We're talking to others

I have a dream, a little, tiny dream
We're all alone
We're left here deserted.

I have a dream, a tiny, little dream
We're cold, wet
We're needing help, oh please.

I have a dream, a little, tiny dream
We're homeless, nowhere to go
We're caring for ill, dying.

I have a dream, a little, tiny dream
We're very thirsty
We're so dehydrated.

I have a dream, a little, tiny dream
We're rich - not
We're quite the opposite.

I have a dream, a tiny, little dream
We're in pain, sore
We're coughing, choking, dying.

I have a dream, a little, tiny dream
We're dying, dying
We're *dead*.

Tanya Watkins (13)
Sandford Middle School, Wareham

Racism

My dream for when my children grow up,
Racism would be stopped.
I don't want my children feeling ashamed,
Ashamed of what they look like.
It is the inside that counts.
The caring, loving and their personalities.

Racists don't think of the people who suffer,
For their children, their family, their friends.
Getting bullied or being called names
All for what they look like.
For people who are racists,
Before you do anything, stop.
Think for the people who look different,
We are all the same.

The world is a horrible place with racists.
Walking around with people getting bullied.

The world would be a better place
With racism coming to a stop.
All the British, Americans, black people,
All coming together in harmony.
The world would be a better place
With nobody getting hurt.
You could feel safe walking down the road.
You would know your child would be safe
When they go outside.

Courtney Critchell (12)
Sandford Middle School, Wareham

The World

Why in the world would people want to change colour
From black to white?
Is there something wrong with this world?
All the poverty, children living on the streets,
Crying out for their mums in the night.
They're so scared; they're running out of light
The world's changing every day
Some ways good and some ways bad
Coming home from school, your house is all smashed up
Parents explaining there's nothing to worry about,
'It's just bad luck, it's in your destiny'
Babies sleeping in cardboard boxes,
All their mums gone away
Daddy's going through the bins looking for a meal
While Mum comes back with baby, both starving with hunger
If one day we could wake up
And all the bad things were so far away,
So far away so that no one knew it existed
To the stars and not back again and everyone forgets
So when it's gone just carry on with our lives,
So every child and pet is wanted
Nobody ever crying
All the water will be clear, everyone full of laughter
A different party every day
Not like now, everyone getting discriminated against,
But if we all help each day we should all be okay
Because when you're walking down the street
You don't want any graffiti on the wall
So everybody stand up and fight this war
Against the bad and evil.

Emily Crocker (13)
Sandford Middle School, Wareham

Poverty

Why should babies and children cry?
Why should babies and children die?
So many people in the world but there's still a drop of silence.
Many tears have flowed down cheeks,
Just for the loss of their loved ones.
Starvation and dehydration have swept many countries in the world,
But what will people do?
What will people say?
When the people care, they turn many lives around,
With food and water for them to survive on.
Instead of screaming and children dying,
There will be laughter and happiness in the air.
They thank those people and they praise them so,
For saving lives in many countries.
All they want is just enough food and water for the world,
Is that too much to ask from people?
Why should babies and children cry?
Why should babies and children die?
Make poverty history.

Rebecca Burt (12)
Sandford Middle School, Wareham

I Had A Dream

You are standing there,
Watching black people being slaved,
Buses, trains and aeroplanes,
Colour doesn't matter,
Being kicked off transport,
Being slaved which causes pain,
Put a stop to it,
Doesn't matter what you look like,
You are all the same,
Just leave them alone,
Stay away from their homes,
We do the same things,
They have no diseases,
If they're poor give them food,
Give a little money for the child's education,
Make a good decision,
Like others.

Briony Wills (12)
Sandford Middle School, Wareham

I Have A Dream

I have a dream
In bed at night
It's not in colour
Only black and white.

I have a dream
It cannot be right
To treat people so different
Because they are black and not white.

I have a dream
Why are people so cruel?
The colour of skin
Makes no difference at all.

I have a dream
I have long blonde hair
Should I be judged by this
Would that really be fair?

I have a dream
No one's the same
We are all very different
Prejudice has nothing to gain.

I have a dream
Just like Martin Luther King
Of fairness and peace
All equality might bring.

I have a dream
Judge me for *me!*
For what I am inside
Not what you can see!

Courtney McCarthy-Dyer (12)
The Cavendish School, Eastbourne

I Have A Dream

I have a dream,
that one day I will soar through the sky like a bird,
so free, willing and able.
I have a dream,
that one day I will be able to help others
that are anguished and hide behind their own tormented shadow,
from their own tortured past.
I have many dreams,
but the most powerful dream is that everyone is happy and peaceful;
and just simply lives a long and happy life.

Nicole Hoddinott (11)
The Cavendish School, Eastbourne

I Had A Dream

I had a dream that children would play without hatred and fear.
I had a dream that animals wouldn't be harmed
and they would be free to play without fear.
I had a dream that hunting would be banned
and all the killing would be stopped.
I had a dream that everyone would live in houses
and no one would be on the streets.
I had a dream that there would be no suffering.
I hope these dreams come true.

Rhianna Dunn (11)
The Cavendish School, Eastbourne